F

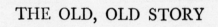

THE OLD, OLD STORY

Uniform with this Volume :

WHAT SHALL I READ ?
The Children's Story of Literature by Edward Albert, M.A.

THE BOOK OF THE WILD
Nature Tales from Many Lands by J. Chappell

DIAMONDS IN THE SKY
by Dr. A. C. D. Crommelin

ARABIAN NIGHTS
A selection of tales

THE WATER BABIES
by Charles Kingsley

THE OLD, OLD STORY

by

W. M. CLOW, D.D.

COLLINS
LONDON AND GLASGOW

First Printed, 1923
Reprinted, 1930
,, 1931
,, 1932
First Printed in this Edition, September, 1939
Reprinted, January, 1943
,, November, 1944

220
648

PRINTED AND MADE IN GREAT BRITAIN BY
WM. COLLINS SONS AND CO. LTD.
LONDON AND GLASGOW

Contents

CONTENTS

List of Illustrations

LIST OF ILLUSTRATIONS

WHEN ALL THE WORLD WAS YOUNG

The Oldest Story in the World

IN the beginning, the very beginning of this oldest story in the world, God, who is our Father in heaven, made this world in which we live. He made it out of nothing, and He made it by speaking word after word. That is how God creates everything. He simply called the whole wide world into being, and He made it to be a home for His children. The swallow builds her nest under the eaves of the houses to hold her nestlings. The bear hollows out a sheltered place and makes it soft and warm for her young ones. A father provides a house to be a home for his children. So God made this great world of earth and sea and sky, not only because He loves to make things beautiful, but because He wanted a place for man to dwell in.

He did not make this world, as we see it and know it, all at once. He began by creating the great round earth, which we know to be a globe in the heavens. But the earth was covered with mist and darkness, and so God said, " Let there be light." Then the mists were rolled away and the darkness was gone. Then He spoke another creating word, and He made

the heavens over our heads like a great wide arch of
blue.   The next thing He did was to gather the
waters together, and make the broad ocean so that
the brown earth stood up above them.   On the
earth there began to spring up tender grass, green
herbs, and trees that might bring forth fruit and give
shade and shelter.   After that He set the sun, the
moon, and the stars to be lights in the heaven, some
for the day-time, and some for the night.   But this
strange new world was silent.   There were no living
creatures in it.   So God created the fish in the sea
and in the rivers, the birds that flew from tree to tree,
and the beasts of the field that wandered far and wide
over the green pastures of the earth.

It was a world of wonder and beauty.   God rejoiced
when He looked upon it and He saw that it was good.
But the world had one great want.   There were no
men and women in it, and no boys and girls.   There
was no one to see it as God saw it, and no one who
could use and delight in all its wealth of good things.
Beyond that, there was no one who could look up to
God and speak to Him.   So God created man.   The
first man God made was called Adam.

We are told that God made him " in His own like-
ness."   That means that Adam was not like any one
of the creatures God had already made.   It means
that he had eyes that could see God, ears that could
hear Him speak, hands that could work for Him,
and a heart that could love Him.   God gave to Adam
a wise mind, for He created him to be the overseer

of all His work, to have dominion over the creatures, and take charge of all else that God had made. He wanted Adam to take such care of the birds and the beasts, and to watch and cultivate all that grew on the face of the earth, so as to make the world still more beautiful, and to be a place of delight to God and of happiness to man.

It was in Arabia, which is now almost a desert.

Now God had prepared a special dwelling-place for Adam. We know whereabouts that dwelling-place was, and where men and women first lived on the earth. It was in Arabia. That land is now almost a desert, although some of the rivers which watered the land are still flowing to the sea. It might still be beautiful if men would only do God's will, and keep it as it should be kept. When God gave Adam this dwelling-place it was a garden, and there is nothing more beautiful, or more delightful, or more full of peace than a garden. Every one would like a garden to keep. "We are nearer God's heart in a garden than anywhere else on earth."

Now we know why God made Adam's dwelling-place to be a garden. It was not only because Adam needed a home, and a place to live in, and to love, in the midst of this broad and empty world. It was not only for Adam's shelter and security. He placed Adam in the garden that he might dress it and keep it. That was the bit of work that God gave Adam to do, and that is one of the most delightful things in the world.

But God put Adam into the garden for another reason. It was to be the special place where God could meet Adam, and be his companion. As we are told, God walked in the garden "in the cool of the day." The cool of the day means that evening hour when the hot sun has gone down, and the shadows are falling, and there is often a deep sense of quiet all around. So God meant the garden to be the place where He could speak to Adam, and hear Adam speak to Him, for God loves the voice of our little human praise.

But this oldest story in the world is not all told when we read of Adam keeping and dressing the Garden of Eden, and having fellowship with God, the Father in heaven. Adam was the only man on the earth. He saw no other human face. He heard no other human voice. God saw how lonely a man he was. " It is not good," God said, " for a man to be alone." If we had no companions, no one to speak to, no one to walk with, no one to play with, how dull would our days be, and how weary we would grow.

So God created a woman to be Adam's companion. He gave her the name of Eve, and Eve means what we all know to be a very dear and beautiful word— the word " mother." She was called Eve, we are told, because she was to be " the mother of all living." So this oldest story in the world ends by telling us of Adam living in the garden, keeping it in order and in beauty, giving all the birds and beasts their names, and caring for them. But the best of it all is that by his side, as his constant helper, there was Eve, his wife, and that both were busy in making the Garden of Eden a home for themselves and their children, and a place where they might serve God.

OUTSIDE THE GATE OF THE GARDEN

Now this beautiful Garden of Eden could be the home and dwelling-place of Adam and Eve only so long as they kept God's commandments. If they had been always true and obedient to their Father in heaven, the story would have been full of delight to read. But they disobeyed God. They refused to keep His laws. They sinned against Him and His goodness, and that spoiled it all.

In the midst of the garden God had planted two trees which were different from all the rest of the trees. God said that they must not touch the fruit of these two trees, although they might pluck and eat as much as they liked of the fruit of all the other trees in the garden.

One of these trees was called the Tree of Life. The other was called the Tree of the Knowledge of Good and Evil. As Adam and Eve walked in the garden, and as they kept it and dressed it, they saw these two forbidden trees every day. But they did not pluck their fruit, because they were content to believe that God was good, and that He did not wish them to eat of the fruit of these trees, for a wise reason.

But the Evil One, who hates God and goodness, is always trying to make us do wrong. He came to Adam and Eve, as we are told, as a serpent might come. The serpent is the most cunning and hateful of all the beasts. He has a poisoned tongue, and when he stings with his tongue, he sends his poison into the wound, until the blood is poisoned and the end is death. So the Evil One, who tempts us all, stung and poisoned the hearts of Adam and Eve.

He spoke to Eve first. He said to her that God had forbidden them to eat of these two trees because He wanted to keep them ignorant. He added that God did not wish them to enter into the fullness of knowledge and power and joy. " In the day ye eat thereof," he said to Eve, " then your eyes shall be opened, and ye shall be as gods, knowing good and evil."

As Eve listened to the tempter's words, she looked again at the tree, and she saw how good it seemed to be, both because good for food and pleasant to the eye. And she thought that if it would make one wise it was a fruit to be desired. She became curious to know if this were true. So she put forth her hand and ate the fruit. Then she gave some to Adam and he also ate it.

In a moment all was changed. Their hearts had been poisoned. They began to know good and evil. The garden was no longer so lovely and so full of delight. They looked upon each other, and they held their heads down in shame.

So when God came to walk in the garden in the cool of the day, He could not find them. Then He called for them, crying, "Where art thou?" But they had hidden themselves in the shadow of the thick-leaved trees. There they cowered in shame and fear. But God did not call because He was angry. He called because He loved them. He was grieved at their sin, and was sorry for all they had lost. But just as a mother seeks a little boy or girl who has gone out into the street or into some dark wood and is lost, so God called, and called again, "Where art thou?" Then, from his hiding-place, Adam said that Eve and he had eaten of the forbidden tree, and that now they were afraid, and had hidden themselves from God's face.

What did God do when He found that Adam and Eve had not been obedient and had eaten the fruit of the forbidden tree ? He turned first to the Evil One who had tempted them, and He passed an awful sentence upon him. He would be nothing but a poisonous and venomous and crawling serpent to the end. He turned to Eve and said that she would have sorrow and pain even when little children came to her, and that life would never be the same as it might have been had she been obedient.

Then He spoke to Adam and told him that he must leave the garden and pass outside its gate to a toilsome life, in a world very different from the lovely Eden they must leave. The earth would now grow thorns and thistles. Adam would need every day to earn his bread in the sweat of his face, and to find that hard labour and strange sorrow would be a part of every day's life.

So Adam and Eve passed out of the garden hand in hand. They built a little hut for their home. They made coats of the skins of the animals they caught for their clothing. They set to work to break up the hard and thorny ground so that in the time of harvest they might have corn to make their daily bread. And God drove them out, and He set angels, with a flaming sword, to keep them back from the Tree of Life.

The old Hebrew scholars tell a lovely story which is not in the Bible, but it may well be true. They say that as Adam and Eve were being driven out of the garden Eve saw a little flower growing just inside the gate. She stooped down and lifted the flower, with its root, and put it in her bosom. She passed out with the hope of planting it in their new and cheerless home. She wanted to keep a flower in remembrance of the wondrous beauty of the garden and the joy of its innocent days. But she had not gone ten steps away into the outer world till the flower withered and died. She was taught that we cannot grow the flowers of Eden outside its gate. We cannot disobey God's word and keep His company and receive His blessing. We must always love and obey.

THE FLOOD AND THE RAINBOW

As time passed on, the great broad plain in which Adam and Eve and Cain and Abel had dwelt became full of people. Some lived in tents and kept sheep. Some grew corn and led their cattle to the pastures. Some built villages and towns, and began to work in brass and iron. They furnished their homes with lovely curtains and carpets, and a passer-by would have heard the songs they sang in the evening. It was a busy world, and it should have been a happy one.

But again the wickedness of men spoiled it all. They were disobedient to God's laws and did not worship Him. They were greedy, and selfish, and quarrelsome, and violence filled the earth. God was angry and vexed at the evil world. So God made up

His mind to destroy this evil world, and to cleanse it by sending a great Flood.

But there was one good man who trusted God, and served Him, with his children and his household. His name was Noah, and we are told that he was " a just man, and upright in his generation, and he walked with God."

Now, one day God spoke to Noah. He told him that the wickedness of the world grieved Him at His heart. He said, " Behold I, even I, do bring a flood of waters upon the earth to destroy all flesh, wherein is the breath of life, from under heaven ; and everything that is in the earth shall die." And He bade Noah build an ark for his shelter and safety when the Flood came. The ark was a large, broad boat, like a great barge. It was divided into many rooms and was covered over with a roof. God told Noah to go out and gather together birds and beasts, and to take them with him into the ark when it was built. When the ark was finished, Noah and his family and all the birds and beasts he had gathered went in through the wide door. And then God shut the door, and Noah waited for the coming of the Flood.

Then the Flood came. The sky grew blacker and blacker with clouds day by day. The air became close and still and stifling. At last the great storm burst over the earth. For forty days and forty nights the rain poured down. The fields were sodden with water. The pools filled and the streams ran in torrents. The great rivers overflowed, and day after day the waters rose higher and higher, until the tops of the loftiest hills were covered.

It was a dreadful, even a horrible sight. The terrified men and women, carrying their helpless children, and the savage animals fleeing from death, fled to the heights to escape the rising flood of waters, and they fought for their lives. At the end of one hundred and fifty days the Flood had covered the whole broad plain, and God's will was fulfilled. The earth was cleansed and the evil-doers, with their wicked haunts, were swept away. But the ark floated safely upon the waters, and Noah and his household and all the beasts he had taken with him were saved alive.

But Noah felt it to be a long and trying time. It must have been trying to be cooped up in so cramped a place as the ark, and Noah and his family grew weary. One day he opened the window, and looked out on the wide-spreading flood. He sent out a raven to see if it could find any place where it could rest. But the raven did not come back. Then he sent out a dove, but the dove came back weary and fluttered in through the window. He waited a short time, and sent out the dove again. Now, the dove brought back a green olive leaf, and Noah knew that, somewhere across the waters, the dry land had begun to appear.

After a few days he sent forth the dove once more. The dove did not come back, so Noah knew that the flood was passing away, and soon the ark would rest upon dry ground. That day came, and Noah, and all with him in the ark, passed out to a new world on which the sun had begun to shine and the cool winds to blow. It was cleansed, and full of beauty and charm.

When we feel grateful to God, or to any man, we should give thanks. That was what Noah did. The place where the ark rested was called Mount Ararat. Noah gathered some of its stones, and he built an altar, and he offered burnt offerings. That was the way in which, in those days, men showed their gratitude to God for His love and care. As Noah and his family kneeled round the altar, and the smoke of the burnt offerings arose in the quiet air, God spoke to Noah. God was pleased at Noah's mindfulness, and He made a great promise, that never again would the earth be destroyed by a flood, but that in mercy He would be patient with men. God said to Noah, " While the earth remaineth, seedtime and harvest, and cold and heat, and summer and winter, and day and night shall not cease."

That night Noah saw a sight of wonderful beauty. A rainbow, with its great arch of many colours, spanned the whole heavens.

We all love the rainbow for its beauty. We shall love it still more for its promise. We say, " A rainbow at night is the shepherd's delight." And a great poet has written, " My heart leaps up when I behold a rainbow in the sky." But we should love it more because it is the token of God's loving-kindness to men.

THE TRAVELLERS IN THE DAWN

THE name of Abraham is one of the great names of the Bible. He was born a long time after Noah. Noah's three sons, Shem, Ham, and Japheth, went out into the cleansed and empty world, and began to cultivate the soil. As the years passed on, the earth again became filled with people. They were busy as before in the work and the life and the joy which are open to us all who live in this world of beauty. They were not so wicked as men had been before God sent the flood. But they did not know God as we know Him now. Some worshipped idols, and others bowed down to the sun and the moon and the stars. No one of them thought of God as the Father in heaven, and the best friend of man.

A part of this broad plain where these strange things happened was named Chaldea, and in Chaldea there was a place named Ur. In this place, known as Ur of the Chaldees, there lived a man whose name was Terah. He was a good man, and he was not content with the life and worship of the people around about him. They built temples, and high towers to watch the movements of the sun and the moon and the stars, and they appointed star-gazers and magicians who tried to foretell the future. Terah wanted to leave this land, but he died before he was able to go very far. But Abraham was his eldest son, and he was a seeker after the true God. He set out from Ur to come into the land of Canaan, and he became known as the man who believed in God.

We are not told much about that great day when Abraham left Ur and its worship of the heavens. But we know certainly what God said to him when He called him. Abraham never forgot God's words.

" Get thee out of thy country, and from thy kindred, and from thy father's house, unto a land that I will show thee: and I will make of thee a great nation, and I will bless thee, and make thy name great; and thou shalt be a blessing."

Abraham believed God's word, and came out of this heathen land, to keep God's fellowship, so that he was known as " the friend of God."

Now we know how Abraham came, for men travel in the East in the same way to-day as they travelled then. He gathered his flocks and his herds, collected his household stock, loaded his camels and folded his tents. Then, in a slow and patient journey, with many stoppings by the way, he travelled out of the valley where he lived, over the hilly lands and on to Damascus, until he came to the dearest land of all, the land of Canaan. There went with him his wife Sarah, and that name has the fine meaning of " a queen." He took also his nephew Lot, for Lot's

father was dead, and there never was a kinder heart
than Abraham's. He passed down through the land
until he came to Shechem. That is the place where,
long afterwards, Jacob digged a well, and where
Jesus spoke with the woman of Samaria.

In the story of Abraham there are many wonderful
things. We shall recall three of them. The first of

He passed through the land until he came to Shechem.

these is this, that wherever Abraham went, and as
often as he removed his camp, he built an altar to
God. He had no Bible to read. He had no Church
into which he could pass and pray. He had no
Sunday to remind him of God's love and power.
There were no other men and women who believed in
God. We are told that " The Canaanite was then

in the land." That means that the people of the
land were wicked idolaters. So Abraham built his
altar, first at Shechem, then at Bethel, where Jacob
afterwards dreamed, then at Hebron, where Abraham
lived for many years. We do not wonder he is called
" the friend of God," and we understand why he was
known as " the father of the faithful."

Another story tells us of a deed of high courage.
The people and the tribes made war in those days
as they do now. They gathered their soldiers and
marched into the countries of their neighbours, and
threw down the walls of the cities, and carried off
precious goods and many captives, and made them
slaves. A band of tribes came down upon Sodom
and Gomorrah, where Lot now lived. They took Lot
and his family captives.

Abraham gathered his servants, went after this
thievish little army, and rescued Lot and the goods
of which he had been despoiled. It was an act of
daring, but it was followed by an action of even
greater beauty. Those who were rescued thought
they would pay Abraham by giving him some of
the possessions he had taken from the raiders. But
Abraham said, " I have lift up mine hand unto the
Lord, that I will not take from a thread even to
a shoe-latchet, and that I will not take anything
that is thine." It is a noble thing to do a kindness
without thought of oneself.

Even more beautiful are those stories of Abraham
which show how often and how tenderly God spoke

The dove brought back a green olive leaf.

(*See page* 11)

Noah, and all with him in the ark, passed out to a new world. (See page 12)

He saw only heaps of ruins still smoking.

(See page 21

to Abraham. It is the simple truth that God spake face to face with him " as a man speaketh to his friend."

There came to him one day an old man weary with travel. Abraham took him into his tent and gave him supper. But the old man began to eat without prayer. He did not ask a blessing. Abraham was angry, and sent him out of the tent into the night and the desert. Then God called to Abraham, and asked him where the stranger was. He said, " I sent him away because he did not worship Thee." God answered, " I have suffered him these many years; couldst not thou suffer him for one night ? " Abraham felt ashamed. He went out and found him. He brought him back, and gave him all that he needed. It was after this fashion, and in this way, that God kept fellowship with His friend, Abraham.

THE DESTRUCTION OF SODOM

A young man whose name was Lot came with Abraham out of the land of the Chaldees. He also lived in tents, and Abraham and Lot kept their flocks and herds together. But their flocks and herds began to increase. There was not room enough and food enough for them all. Then the herdsmen of Lot began to quarrel with the herdsmen of Abraham. When they drew water from the wells, and when they chose the quiet resting-places for the night, angry strife broke out between them.

Abraham was deeply grieved. He took Lot one day up to a high place from which they could see all over the land. He asked Lot to choose which part of it he wished for his flocks. He said to Lot, " Is not the whole land before thee ? Separate thyself, I pray thee, from me ; if thou wilt take the left hand, then I will go to the right ; but if thou wilt depart to the right hand, then I will go to the left."

So the two men stood and looked out over the land. On one side there were the hill pastures of Canaan. On the other side there was the deep valley of the Jordan. It had fields of living green and a wealth of flowers where the bees gathered their honey. It was as lovely as Eden, as the garden of the Lord. Lot did not think twice. His greedy heart desired this fruitful land. So he chose it, and left Abraham only the fields of the high uplands of Canaan.

Lot's selfish choice was neither kind nor wise. For one thing, he was breaking his friendship and companionship with Abraham. He was separating himself from the best man he had ever known. He was turning his back on the man who had taught him to believe in God. And he was choosing to live among the worst men and women in the world. We are told that " Lot dwelled in the cities of the plain, and pitched his tent towards Sodom." Sodom was a city whose men and women were wicked, and sinners before the Lord exceedingly. But Lot saw only the fertile lands and the never-failing springs, and he set his heart on the riches he might gain.

Abraham and Lot now lived a long way from each other, so that Abraham did not often hear how it fared with Lot. But one day, as Abraham sat in his tent door out of the heat of the midday sun, suddenly three men stood before him. He rose up and bowed himself to them and gave them a word of welcome. He ran and brought them water to wash their dusty feet. Then Sarah prepared a meal, and Abraham

The two men looked out over the land.

spread a table beneath a shady tree, and gave them refreshing food. When the three men had eaten and were rested, they rose up to go on their journey, and Abraham went with them a part of the way.

He found that they were going to Sodom, and that they were messengers of God. They told Abraham that God could bear no longer with the sinful men and women of Sodom and Gomorrah. The wickedness of these cities had come up into God's ears like a loud rebel cry. But God had sent these angel messengers to see the cities, and to inquire if they were so hopelessly evil. Abraham knew how true the report was. He foresaw the awful punishment that would fall upon Sodom. Then he remembered Lot and Lot's household, and stood still in his sorrow. Then, looking upward, he prayed to God to spare Sodom.

God said he would not destroy Sodom if ten good men were found in it. But Abraham knew that there were only four, and he came back to his tent cast down and afraid.

The angel messengers passed on and entered in through the gate of Sodom, and Lot received them into his home. But they found that Sodom was worse even than they expected. Its streets were thronged that night by men who were as vile as evil beasts. These angel messengers knew that God's judgment would fall upon the city, and they entreated Lot and his family to come out and escape to the hills. Lot was not willing, but in the morning the angels laid their hands on the wrists of Lot and his family, and compelled them to come with them.

They escaped only in time. Fire fell from heaven. Fierce flames shot up from the earth. All that day and night the fire continued, and in the morning the city was burned to ashes. In the morning Abraham stood on the heights and looked down into the valley where Sodom and Gomorrah had stood with their beautiful gardens and running streams, and he saw only heaps of ruins still smoking with the fire of their burning. He knew, with a tender sorrow, how foolish had been Lot's choice.

THE OBEDIENCE OF ISAAC

When Abraham and Sarah came into Canaan they had no children. No little boys and girls played at the tent door. No young voices called to them in the morning. That was their sorrow. But Abraham was still sadder, because he had no son to follow him as a true and steadfast believer in God. He was God's friend, and God was his friend, and he deeply desired to have a son who would grow up to serve God as he himself had done. So it was a great joy both to Abraham and to Sarah when a little son was born, and they called him by the name of Isaac.

Isaac was a quiet, gentle, sweet-tempered boy. He found one of his chief delights in walking in the fields. All the loveliness that grew round about him gave him pleasure. He loved his home and kept its customs with a sweet content. He was always tender to his mother, and when she died he had days of grief. He knew his father to be the best man who ever lived, and he never disobeyed him. Beyond all this, he grew up to believe in God, and Abraham had his happiest hours in thinking that when he himself would die and be buried, young Isaac would be true to God and keep His commandments.

So Isaac grew up through boyhood to young

manhood and lived the simple life of the home in Hebron. Then there came a strange and sudden trial. God put Abraham's faith in Him to a hard and vexing proof. He spoke to Abraham and called him and said to him, " Take now thy son, thine only son Isaac, whom thou lovest, and get thee into the land of Moriah ; and offer him there for a burnt offering upon one of the mountains which I will tell thee of."

It was a dreadful trial. Abraham wondered if that could be the command of God. He spent weary days in thinking about it, and sleepless nights heartbroken with sorrow. But he could not, and he would not, disobey God. He took some of his servants, and chose out an ass from his fields to carry their food, and set off on the long journey to Mount Moriah, which is near Jerusalem. When the little company came to the foot of the hill, they left the young men who had gone with them there. Abraham laid the wood he had brought for the fire upon Isaac's strong young shoulders, and then he took a vessel with fire in it to kindle the wood, and a knife in his hand, and began to climb the hill with Isaac.

When they came to the top of the hill they gathered the stones and made the altar. Then they laid the wood, stick upon stick, so as to burn quickly and hotly. Then Isaac laid himself down, and Abraham bound him on the wood. Then came the moment of anguish. He took the knife, and was about to kill Isaac in the same way as men killed the lamb in the sacrifice. But the angel of the Lord called to him out of heaven, and the knife dropped from his hand. God did not want him to slay his son. All God asked was that Abraham would keep back nothing that was dear to him from God when God asked it. And so the angel said, " Lay not thine hand upon the lad, neither do thou anything unto him : for now I know that thou fearest God, seeing thou hast not withheld thy son, thine only son, from Me."

Now we have been thinking about the trial of Abraham, and it was a sore trial to one who loved Isaac as he did. But we must not forget the wonderful obedience of Isaac. He was young, and it is hard for any one who is young even to think of dying. He was full of delight in life, and in all the beauty of the world round about him. He had been dreaming a boy's dreams and wondering about his future when he would have his own home. Then it must have been a very dark and troubling thing to be told that God, who was righteous, was calling on his father to slay him. Yet such was his obedience that without a struggle, and without a word, he laid himself down and offered himself for the sacrifice.

That simple obedience was seen all through Isaac's life. He did not do deeds of daring and adventure, but he was always obedient, keeping in his heart the memory of his father and mother, and leading the flocks about as Abraham had done. And when he was an old man, blind and dying on his bed, he knew that the best gift he could give to his children was the blessing of God, whom he had obeyed.

ESAU AND JACOB

When Isaac grew to be a man he married Rebekah, who came from that far-off land which Abraham had left to dwell in Canaan. They had two sons, Esau and Jacob. The two boys were twins, and twins are often very like each other in every way. But Esau and Jacob were quite unlike one another. Esau was a strong, active boy, keen on adventures. He had a shock of hair on his head, and hair grew thickly upon his neck and his hands. He was skilful with the bow and arrow, and he hunted the deer on the hillside, and brought home its flesh, and his mother dressed the venison, because Isaac was fond of it.

Jacob was not so strong in body or so swift of foot. He was a quiet boy, with a smooth skin, and he found his work in keeping the sheep in the pasture. The two boys were different from each other in their minds. Esau was wild and thoughtless, and did not care for the worship of the home. Esau was the first-born, and had the first right to the blessing, but Jacob deeply desired it.

One day Esau came in from his hunting, hot and tired and faint with hunger. Jacob was cooking a pot of red lentil pottage, at the tent door. Esau's keen eyes gleamed at the sight of the red pottage, and its savoury smell tempted his hunger. He asked Jacob to give him some of this tempting food. But Jacob offered to make a bargain with him.

Jacob said, " Sell me this day thy birthright."

Esau replied, " Behold I am at the point to die ; and what profit shall this birthright do to me ? "

But Jacob was not sure that Esau would keep his word, so he said, " Swear to me this day."

Esau made the solemn promise, and sold the birthright. He ate his mess of pottage with greedy hunger, and rose up and went his way without thinking much about it. Thus Esau despised his birthright, and that meant that he despised the blessing of God.

As the years passed by Esau hardly remembered the day when he had sold his birthright, but Jacob did not forget. Isaac was growing old and feeble, and his eyes were dim that he could not see. So he made up his mind to bestow the blessing, and he meant to give it to Esau. He sent Esau to hunt the deer, and to bring home and prepare some venison that he might eat it, and be strengthened.

His wife Rebekah heard him speaking to Esau. Esau was Isaac's favourite, but Rebekah loved Jacob. She saw that if Isaac blessed Esau, Jacob would lose the birthright after all. She called Jacob and said that he should go in to Isaac and pretend to be Esau, and get the blessing before Esau came back. Jacob said that perhaps Isaac would put out his hand and feel him, and he would discover that he was not hairy-skinned as Esau was, and then he would curse him. Rebekah told him to take two kids of the flock, and she would prepare their flesh to taste like venison, and she would cover his neck and hands with their hairy skins, as well as put Esau's raiment upon him.

So Jacob went in and knelt before his father. But Isaac wondered that Esau had come back so soon. He thought the voice was the voice of Jacob, and when he put out his hand and felt him he said, " The voice is Jacob's voice, but the hands are the hands of Esau." But he lifted up his hands, and called down God's richest blessing on Jacob.

Jacob had hardly gone out from his father when Esau came in with his savoury venison. He knelt down and prayed his father to eat of it, and then to bless him. The poor old blind man was amazed and he cried out, " Who art thou ? " Esau said, " I am thy son, thy first-born son, Esau." Then Isaac trembled exceedingly. He knew that he had given the blessing, with all its promises, to Jacob, and that blessing could not be taken back.

Esau broke out in prayers and tears. But Isaac said that he had given the blessing to Jacob, and it could not be taken back. Esau cried again, " Bless me, even me also, O my father. Hast thou but one blessing, my father ? " Isaac lifted his hands and blessed him, but he could not give the birthright.

Esau went out bitterly angry. He knew that he had sold the birthright simply for a meal of red lentils, only to please himself in a moment of greedy appetite. He did not really care about the blessing of God, but he thought that Isaac's prayer might bring him earthly happiness and worldly power. Isaac's words to him were kind, and did bring him some promise of success in the world. Yet Esau knew that in the

days to come Jacob would follow Isaac, and God
would be known as the God of Abraham and of Isaac
and of Jacob—not as the God of Esau. Deep in
his heart Esau made up his mind that he would kill
Jacob. He would not slay him until his father was
dead, but then he would meet him by the way and
put him to death. It is a sad story, and sadder still

Esau went out bitterly angry.

when we remember that Isaac and Rebekah had to
send Jacob away. Esau's anger might have broken
out at any time, and Rebekah never saw Jacob, her
beloved son, again.

JACOB'S DREAM

Jacob had gained the blessing of the birthright
through the deceit that his mother, Rebekah, had
bidden him practise on Isaac. But he knew that he

had gained the blessing in a wrong way, and he found that everything we gain in a wrong way is followed by some punishment. The fierce anger of Esau grew hotter, and his threats to kill Jacob were well known. So Isaac and Rebekah thought it wiser to send Jacob away out of Esau's sight. So he had to leave his father and mother, and the pleasant home in Hebron, and the land of Canaan, and go to that far-off country from which his mother had come.

So Jacob set out along the high road that leads to the north. All the long day he walked on mile after mile. He had sad thoughts, and he began to see what he had lost, and to be sorry for his evil conduct. He saw himself to be an outcast and a wanderer on the earth. As the sun was setting, and the darkness falling round about him, he came to Bethel. It was a wild and lonely place. The great rocks rose up in terraces on the hillside. Their white stones seemed to be a pathway up to heaven. The clear dark sky over his head was shining with a multitude of stars.

He was young, and well used to hardship. He had often slept in the open air all night, as he had kept his father's sheep. So he took a stone and laid it down for a pillow. He wrapt himself in his cloak and lay down to rest. His thoughts went back to his home, and his father and his mother. They went farther back still, to Abraham who had built an altar at this same place of Bethel, and given it its name, and he must have been thinking how unlike he was to that beloved friend of God.

After a while he fell asleep, and as he slept he dreamed. In his dream he saw a stairway set up on the hillside and reaching right up to heaven. On this stairway the angels of God were passing up and down. They were God's messengers going out from, and coming back to, His presence. At the top of the stairway, high up in the heavens, above all, Jacob saw a vision of God himself. As he lay deep in sleep the dream seemed a reality, as dreams often do, and he heard God say,—

" I am the Lord God of Abraham, and the God of Isaac ; the land whereon thou liest, to thee will I give it, and to thy seed. And thy seed shall be as the dust of the earth ; and thou shalt spread abroad to the west, and to the east, and to the north, and to the south ; and in thee and in thy seed shall all the families of the earth be blessed. And behold, I am with thee, and will keep thee in all places whither thou goest, and will bring thee again into this land."

These were wonderful words, and most wonderful to Jacob, because they promised what he had coveted, and they promised it, just when he feared that he had lost God's blessing altogether. When he awoke he found it was only a dream. But he knew that God often spake to men in dreams, and he was sure that this was the voice of God speaking to him, and assuring him, that he would follow in the steps of his father Isaac and his grandfather Abraham.

He was afraid ; not with the fear of a coward, but with that awe and trembling which the presence of

God and the voice of God should give to every one. So he said, " Surely the Lord is in this place ; and I knew it not. How dreadful is this place ! This is none other but the house of God, and this is the gate of heaven." He had been thinking that God was to be known only in Hebron. Now he knew that where-ever any one thinks about God, or prays to God, there God will answer.

Jacob rose up with a glad and grateful heart. He felt that this place would always be dear to him, and he wanted to mark it, as we do, with some kind of memorial. He took the stone which he had laid down for a pillow, and set it upright, with other stones to support it. Then he poured oil on the top of it, which was the way that men, at that time, set apart themselves, and anything dear to them, as holy to God. He set up this stone to mark the place where he saw the vision of God and heard His voice. In this way when he left Bethel, and wandered far from it, he could think back, and see the white stone standing on the hillside, and that would help him to remember how forgiving God had been.

But he did something more than set up the stone. He vowed a vow and made a covenant with God. He was going out to a strange land, and to live among people whom he had not seen. He was not sure how he would fare among the people he was going to visit. So he said, " If God will be with me, and will keep me in this way that I go, and will give me bread to eat and raiment to put on, so that I come again to my

father's house in peace, then shall the Lord be my God."
That is not the highest kind of vow.   We should serve
God whatever happens to us.

But it was a brave and wise covenant, and it was
beautiful in one way, that it showed Jacob's love for
his home and the land of his father. His deepest
desire was to " come again to his father's house in
peace." He lived for many years in the land called
Padan-aram, but his heart was always in the land
promised to him and his children.

JOSEPH, THE BOY WITH THE COAT OF MANY COLOURS

When Jacob came back to live in Canaan he was
a rich man with many flocks and herds. He had
twelve sons. Reuben and Simeon and Judah were
the eldest of them. Joseph and Benjamin were the
youngest. Jacob loved Joseph more than all his
children. His other sons were dressed in dark-
coloured garments, but for Joseph he made a lovely
robe, with stripes of white and blue and crimson.
He was a sunny-faced, sweet-tempered, most likeable
boy. But his brothers hated him because his father
foolishly favoured him, and the sight of his coat of
many colours made them angry, and they would not
speak peaceably to him.

For another reason they disliked him still more.
He often dreamed at night, and he told his brothers
two of his dreams. In one dream he saw his sheaf
standing upright in the field, and all the sheaves

gathered by his brothers bowed down to his sheaf. In another dream he saw the sun and the moon and the eleven stars bending before him in his honour. He told them these dreams, and his father was displeased and rebuked him, but his brothers were filled with anger. They said," Shalt thou indeed reign over us?"

A short time afterwards Joseph's brothers led the flocks and herds a long way off for the sake of the pasture. Jacob had no word from them, so he sent Joseph to find them, and to bring him back news of the flock. After some trouble, Joseph found them in a valley named Dothan. When they saw his gleaming robe coming down the hillside, their anger became hot within them, and they said in scorn, " Behold, this dreamer cometh ! " They made up their minds to kill him and cast his body into a pit, and tell Jacob that a wild beast had devoured him. But Reuben did not wish to kill him. He said that they should cast him into a pit in the meantime, for he hoped he could find some way to deliver him. So when Joseph came to them they stripped off his coat of many colours, and cast him into the pit.

Then they sat down to their meal. As they were eating, a company of Ishmaelite merchantmen, with a caravan of camels, loaded with spices and other costly things, passed by. They were going down to Egypt. Judah said that they might sell Joseph to these merchants. They took him up out of the pit, and sold him for twenty pieces of silver. The merchant-men passed on their way, taking Joseph with them.

His wicked brothers dipped his coat of many colours in the blood of a kid. They took it back with them to Jacob, and when Jacob saw it he rent his clothes in his grief, and he could not be comforted. He said, as he wept for Joseph, " I will go down into the grave unto my son mourning."

The merchants took Joseph to the slave market, and he was sold to Potiphar, the captain of the guard

Judah said they might sell Joseph.

of Pharaoh, the king of Egypt. Potiphar saw that young Joseph was willing to work, and was honest and faithful. He gave him charge over his household and trusted him with his goods. But a false and wicked story was told to Potiphar about Joseph. Potiphar was very angry, for he believed the story to be true, and he bound Joseph with cords and cast him into the prison.

It was a dark day to Joseph, and his face was sad

when the prison door shut behind him. But he did not brood or sulk. He did not lose hope, because he felt sure that God would care for him. He was helpful and obliging and kind. The keeper of the prison saw this, and in a short time he gave Joseph a charge to take care of the other prisoners with him.

One day there came in two new prisoners, and they were given, as a chief care, to Joseph. One of these prisoners was the butler of the king of Egypt, who waited at his table. The other was the baker of the king of Egypt, who made his bread and his cakes. After they had been some months in the prison and Joseph had begun to know them, he found them one morning dull in spirit and sad in their looks.

He asked them, " Wherefore look ye so sadly to-day ? " They told him that they had each dreamed a dream, but there was no one in the prison who could interpret it.

Joseph said, " Do not interpretations belong to God ? Tell me your dreams, I pray you ? "

The chief butler told him that in his dream he saw a vine with three branches, and these branches brought forth buds and blossoms, and at last ripe grapes. He pressed the grapes into Pharaoh's wine cup, and then gave Pharaoh the cup into his hand. Then said Joseph that this dream meant that in three days Pharaoh would send for the butler and restore him to his service, and he would wait at Pharaoh's table as before.

The chief baker then told his dream. He said that

in his dream he had three white baskets on his head
full of bake-meats for Pharaoh. But some birds flew
down and ate the bake-meats out of the uppermost
basket. Then said Joseph, " These three baskets are
three days, and within three days Pharaoh will take
you and hang you on a tree, and the birds shall eat
your flesh."

That came to pass. Ou the third day, which was
Pharaoh's birthday, he made a feast, and he called
upon the butler to serve him with his wine, but he
hanged the chief baker. Yet Joseph remained in the
prison. He had told the butler that he had been
stolen away from the land of Canaan, and sold as a
slave, and that he had done nothing wrong, so that
he was unjustly put into the dungeon of the prison.
He besought the chief butler to make mention of him
to Pharaoh that he might be brought out of the
prison house. But the chief butler was so happy in
his own freedom, and in being restored to his place
of honour, that he did not remember Joseph, but forgot
him.

JOSEPH, THE RULER IN EGYPT

For two long years Joseph was kept in the prison,
forgotten by every one. Then Pharaoh, the king,
dreamed a strange dream. He dreamed that he saw
seven well-favoured and fat-fleshed cattle feeding in
a meadow near the river. Then he saw seven other
cattle, lean and ill-favoured, coming up out of the

river and standing beside the others. But these lean cattle attacked the well-favoured cattle and ate them up. Then Pharaoh awoke in wonder. He fell asleep again, and dreamed that he saw a stalk of corn on which seven full and rich ears grew. Then seven other ears, thin and poor, and nipped by the east wind, came up after them. Strangely enough, the seven thin ears ate up the seven full and good ears. When he arose from his bed he sent for the magicians and the wise men and he asked them the meaning of his dream, but they could not tell him. So his spirit was greatly troubled, for he felt sure that some evil was to happen to his kingdom.

Then the chief butler suddenly remembered Joseph, and felt ashamed that he had forgotten him. He told Pharaoh about Joseph, and how he had interpreted his own dream and the dream of the chief baker. He said to Pharaoh that all came to pass as this young Hebrew had said. So Pharaoh sent for Joseph. They brought him at once out of the prison, although Joseph asked time to wash himself and to change his raiment, that he might appear in a proper dress before King Pharaoh.

Joseph came into Pharaoh's presence and bowed before him, and Pharaoh told him his two dreams. But Joseph did not pretend, like the magicians, that he could interpret dreams, for he knew that God alone could make him wise. So he said to Pharaoh, " It is not in me : God shall give Pharaoh an answer of peace." Joseph then told Pharaoh the meaning of the dreams.

The seven well-favoured cattle were seven years of plenty, when there would be an abundance of corn. The seven lean cattle would be seven years, when the east wind would blight the corn and they would be years of famine. All the abundance of the seven years of plenty would be eaten up by the seven years of famine, and unless care was taken the people would starve.

Pharaoh listened with an anxious mind. Then Joseph went on to tell Pharaoh what should be done. He should appoint a man who was wise and thoughtful and make him Governor over the whole land of Egypt. He should gather all the food of the good years, and store it up in large barns, and serve it out to the people who were pressed with hunger, and threatened with starvation and death during the seven years of scarcity and famine.

Pharaoh had been looking at Joseph all the time with steadfast eyes. He saw that this must be the true interpretation, and he knew that Joseph was prudent and modest and honest. So he made him the Governor of the land, next to himself in power. He took off his ring and put it on Joseph's hand, dressed him in fine linen, and put a gold chain about his neck, and gave him a chariot to ride in. Then Joseph, as the Governor of Egypt, gathered the corn in all the seven years until there was abundance of provision.

This famine of seven years long, when the crops failed, prevailed also in the land of Canaan. Jacob and his family had no food for their cattle, or for

themselves, but they heard that there was corn in
Egypt. So Jacob sent his ten sons with their asses,
and sacks bound upon their backs, and a large sum of
money to buy corn from the Governor of Egypt, to
keep themselves and their cattle alive. He sent his
ten older sons, but kept Benjamin, the youngest, at
home, for he had never forgotten the loss of Joseph,
and still sorrowed for him.

So these ten brethren came down to Egypt, and
when Joseph saw them he knew them at once, but
they did not know him. They could not think that
this Governor with his fine raiment, and his large
household, and his power, was the boy whose coat of
many colours they had dipped in the blood of the
kid, when they had put him into the pit. Joseph
spoke roughly to them, and said that they were spies.
They said humbly that they were honest men, and
sons of a good father whose name was Jacob. Then
Joseph asked them about Jacob and they told him.
He next asked them about their brothers, and they
said that one of the twelve was not in the father's
house, but that the youngest, Benjamin, had been
left behind, because his father would not send him.

Then Joseph said that he would prove the truth
of their story. They would go back and bring this
youngest brother to him. At first he said he would
let one go back, and keep the other nine in prison.
Then, to be kind to them, he said that nine might go
back, and one stay with him, while the others carried
the corn back for the time of famine. When these

brethren heard this, they looked upon each other, and they said that this was the punishment God was giving them for having done so great a wrong to the boy, Joseph.

They left Egypt with sacks full of corn. Joseph had given orders to put every man's money into the mouth of his sack, and when one of them opened his sack to feed his ass he saw the money lying. Then they all cried out with fear, for they were sure that this Governor who spake so roughly to them would say that they had stolen the money. But they pressed on to Canaan, and when they opened their sacks they saw the little bundle of the money in the mouth of every sack, and they were all afraid. But Jacob refused to let Benjamin go. He said, " My son shall not go down with you, for his brother is dead, and he is left alone." Then they replied that they would not go back again unless Benjamin went with them.

After a while, when they had eaten all the corn, they said to their father that they must go down again to Egypt, and Benjamin must go with them. So he consented, and this time they took double money in their hands, and a present for the Governor, of balm and honey and spices. When Joseph saw Benjamin his heart was moved. He took the whole company to his house, and they went in with fear and trembling. They told him that they had not stolen the money, and they answered his questions about their father until Joseph had to leave the room to hide his tears. Then he made them a feast, and he sent a special portion to Benjamin, and after the feast they were sent away.

This time Joseph told his steward to fill the sacks with food, and to put every man's money in the sack's mouth, and to put his own silver cup in Benjamin's sack. Then he was to follow after them, and charge them with having stolen the Governor's cup. All this was done, and when the cup was found in Benjamin's sack they rent their clothes, came back to the Governor, and fell down before him in shame and fear. Then Joseph saw that they were really sorry for the wrong they had done, and that they were true men, so he told them who he was. They were amazed. He kissed them all and comforted them. Then he sent for his father and brought the whole household down to Egypt, and they had abundant food in the years of the famine.

THROUGH THE GREAT WILDERNESS

Moses in Pharaoh's Household

WHEN Jacob came into Egypt, with his sons and their children, he meant to go back to Canaan when the years of famine were over. But King Pharaoh showed him great kindness, and Joseph gave them fertile fields for their flocks. So they stayed on in Egypt, and had children and grandchildren born to them. Only seventy, counting old and young, came into Egypt, but soon they became a great people.

As time passed on, Jacob and Joseph, and the king who was so kind to them, all died. A new king was on the throne, who began to fear the Hebrew people, and he oppressed them. He made them slaves. He set them to toil on the land, and in the brickfields, and in building him cities. He put hard taskmasters over them, and they made the lives of the people bitter by their cruelty. Then the king made an order that every baby boy born should be thrown into the river, and only the baby girls should be kept alive. The poor Hebrew people were wretched and miserable.

Now there was a Hebrew family who kept a firm faith in God. The father's name was Amram and the mother's name was Jochebed. A little son was born to them. They had two older children, a daughter called Miriam and a son called Aaron. The baby born to them was a beautiful child, and his mother felt that he must not be thrown into the river. So she hid him for three months. It was not easy to keep the little one from being seen, or his baby voice from being heard, and it was sad for the child never to be out in the morning air, and the sweet sunshine. But for three months she kept the baby in her home.

But, as the child grew, his mother knew that he could not be hidden any longer. So she made an ark of bulrushes. It was a basket which she covered with cloth, and she daubed it with tar, so that it might float on the river, and the water would not go through. Then she put the child into the little ark, and covered him up. At night she took the basket down to the river, and set it afloat on the water among the reeds and rushes. She was very anxious in mind, for a crocodile might crush the basket with his strong teeth, or the little child might struggle out of it, and fall into the river. So she set his sister, Miriam, to stand some distance away, and to watch what happened to the ark.

In the morning King Pharaoh's daughter came down to bathe in the river, and a company of maidens came with her, to wait upon her. As she was stepping into the water she saw the ark among the bulrushes, and she sent one of her maids to fetch it. When she opened the covering which Jochebed had put over the ark, she found the little child, and she saw that the child was weeping. Pharaoh's daughter was kind-hearted, and she was sorry for the babe. She guessed at once how the ark had been made, and why it had been put into the water, and she said, " This is one of the Hebrews' children."

As she was wondering what she would do with the little child, Miriam, who had been watching all the time with a beating heart, came up to her and asked, " Shall I go and call to thee a nurse of the Hebrew women, that she may nurse the child for thee ? " Pharaoh's daughter saw that this was a wise plan, and she said to her, " Go." Miriam ran off to her mother's house, and told her mother how the babe had been found. She brought her mother back to Pharaoh's daughter, and she was given the little child into her arms, with great joy. Pharaoh's daughter said to her, never thinking that she was the boy's mother, " Take this child away, and nurse it for me, and I will give thee thy wages."

So it came about that the child lived in his father's house and grew up at his mother's knee. The first things he learned were the name of God, and the stories of God's goodness to the Hebrews and all the promises God had made to Abraham and to Isaac and to Jacob. But when he grew old enough, Pharaoh's daughter sent for him, and he lived with her in the king's household. She treated him as though he were her own child, and he was called " the son of Pharaoh's daughter." She named him Moses because he had been drawn out of the water.

It was a great change for Moses to be taken from the little narrow home of his father and mother beside the River Nile, to live in the splendid palace of the king. He might have been only a Hebrew slave, toiling in a hot sun under a pitiless Egyptian taskmaster. He became a prince in Pharaoh's house. So it came to pass that he was educated in all the wisdom of the Egyptians, and they were the most learned people of the time. He read their books. He was taught their history. He came to know their ways of life, and the manner of their feasts and their funerals, and he began to understand their skill as workmen in stone and iron.

The Egyptian people began to think that one day he would sit upon the throne and be the king of Egypt. But he did not forget his father and his mother and what they had taught him. He knew the Egyptians to be heathens. They worshiped the sun, and the moon, and the stars. Sometimes they bowed down to the crocodiles, and even to the cats, which they held to be sacred, and Moses had no part with them in that foolishness.

One day he went out among the people and saw how heavy were their burdens and how hard was their bondage. He came upon an Egyptian taskmaster cruelly lashing a Hebrew slave. In his anger he slew the taskmaster and hid his body in the sand. On the next day he found two Hebrews quarrelling and fighting, and he checked them. One of them said to him, " Wilt thou kill me as thou killedst the Egyptian ? " Moses was amazed that it was known that he had killed the Egyptian. He learned that King Pharaoh had heard of it, and was sending men to kill him. So Moses fled out of Egypt. He had become the defender and protector of the Hebrew people, and he took his stand with them. As it was said of him long afterwards, " Moses chose rather to suffer affliction with the people of God than to enjoy the pleasures of sin for a season."

MOSES, THE SHEPHERD OF HOREB

Moses knew how hot with anger Pharaoh was because he had killed the Egyptian. He was sure that he would search far and near for him. So he fled away to Midian, a land in the north country, where there were wide and trackless deserts, with few people living in them. He did not stop in his journey until he came to a well. He sat down by the well to rest. He was both sad and weary, and had begun to wonder if he did right to be so angry, and to be sorry that he had been so hot-tempered as to slay the Egyptian taskmaster.

In this land of Midian there lived a man who kept his flocks near the well. His name was Jethro, and he had seven daughters. As Moses sat by the well, they came to it to draw water and to fill the troughs out of which the sheep, so thirsty in that hot and desert land, used to drink. But some rough and selfish shepherd men came up, and behaved rudely to Jethro's daughters, and drove their sheep away from the well. Moses at once stood up and defended the daughters of Jethro, and he helped them to water their flock. When they went back to their father's tent, they told him how they had been treated, and how this young stranger had defended them and helped them. Jethro sent out and brought him into his tent, and set him down at his table.

Year after year passed away, yet Moses felt himself to be a stranger in a strange land. He could not forget Egypt, and his father and mother, and he often remembered the Hebrew people. He did not know that the king who had tried to kill him was dead. Nor did he know that the Hebrew people were suffering even a harder bondage and a crueller lot than before. Had he been in Egypt, he would have heard their cries in their distress.

One day he led his flock away to a lonely spot behind a high mountain called Horeb. As he prayed to God he saw a strange sight. A bush began to flame with fire, yet the bush was not burned. Moses wondered at this, and he went aside to see if he could find out why the bush was not burned in the flame. Then God called to him out of the bush, and said, "Moses, Moses." And Moses said, "Here am I." Then God spoke again. "Draw not nigh hither; put off thy shoes from off thy feet, for the place whereon thou standest is holy ground." As Moses obeyed this command and stood still, God said, " I am the God of thy father, the God of Abraham, the God of Isaac, and the God of Jacob." Then Moses veiled his face, for he was afraid to look upon God.

As Moses bowed down, not lifting up his eyes, God

He helped them to water their flock.

told Moses that he should go back to Egypt and become the leader of the people, for they had no one in Egypt who could help them. Moses heard this message with fear, and he said, " Who am I, that I should go unto Pharaoh, and that I should bring forth the children of Israel out of Egypt ? "

When Moses came back to Egypt, he sought out Aaron, and asked his help. Then he called the people

together and gave them God's message. Along with
Aaron he went boldly to Pharaoh, and besought him
to let the people go, only for three days into the
wilderness to worship God. Pharaoh was in a rage
and he refused. He doubled the burdens on the poor
enslaved Israelites. So God sent dreadful plagues
upon the Egyptians. The River Nile was turned into
blood. Swarms of frogs and lice, of flies and of locusts,
made life a misery. Their cattle died of horrible
diseases, and boils broke out on their own bodies.
Hail storms smote the land and hours of darkness
blackened the sky. But Pharaoh's wicked heart was
hardened. He would not let the people go.

God's long patience was spent. He told Moses that
one more stroke would smite the Egyptians. The
first-born of every man and of every beast would die
that night. So He bade Moses to command the people
to gather in silence in their houses, all dressed and
ready for the journey. Each family must take a
lamb and slay it. Its blood must be sprinkled on the
posts of the door. Its flesh must be eaten as the family
stood round the table. So, as they ate, God's Angel of
death flew over the homes of the people. The first-born
was smitten, and a great cry of sorrow rang through
the land. But when God's Angel saw the blood
sprinkled on the door-posts, he " passed over " the
houses of the Israelites, and no one was slain. Then
Pharaoh came in an awful terror, and bade the people
go at once, and they marched out in a new faith in God.

Now God commanded the people never to forget this

Pharaoh listened with an anxious mind.

(*See page* 37)

D

" Alas, my daughter !"
(See page 72)

He made them slaves.

(*See page* 41)

night, and to celebrate it by observing a Passover Feast. So, when the boys and girls saw the preparations being made, the little lamb brought in from the fold—perhaps they were sent to bring it—and when they saw it slain and eaten they would ask, " What mean ye by this service ? " Then they would be told the story of this last night in Egypt. They would rejoice with their fathers and mothers, and begin to understand God's love and care of His people.

THE CROSSING OF THE RED SEA

On that never to be forgotten night in Egypt when God slew the first-born children, from the first-born of Pharaoh on the throne to the first-born of the prisoner in the dungeon, a great cry rang through the land. It was the cry of the people lamenting their dead, and looking on their faces with a new dread of the children of Israel.

Pharaoh rose in the darkness of the night, and sent for Moses and Aaron. He was terrified, with all the people, for the troubles which had fallen upon the land. The nine plagues had made life miserable, but this last stroke smote every one with terror. So Pharaoh said to Moses and Aaron, " Rise up, and get you forth from among my people, both ye and the children of Israel ; and go, serve the Lord, as ye have said." The people came to the children of Israel in their anxiety to get them out of the land, and gave them jewels of gold and of silver, and much raiment, and besought them to depart at once. So the children of Israel took all that they had, their sheep and their cattle, and even their cooking vessels, and when the morning light had come, they passed out, a great host of people, into the wilderness.

Their purpose was to go back to Canaan, from which Jacob and his sons had come. But the most direct and shortest road had many dangers. So God told Moses to lead the people about by a longer way. They were to march out into the wilderness, and go down to the shore of the Red Sea, and continue their journey around the end of it, and in that way pass into the trackless desert, where they would be safe from Pharaoh and his host. He gave them a pillar of cloud to go before them in their journey. It was white, like a column of smoke in the daytime, but it glowed like fire in the darkness of the night.

As soon as they were gone, and Egypt was left behind, with their empty homes, King Pharaoh changed his mind. He called his soldiers together, with their horses, and he made ready six hundred chariots, and set captains over them. He prepared his own chariot, and rode out in it at the head of this armed company. They pursued after the children of Israel, and overtook them as they were encamped on the bank of the Red Sea.

The noise of this great host fell upon the ears of the people, and when they lifted up their eyes they saw the men and the chariots sweeping down upon them. They were unarmed men, helpless women, and little children, and they were smitten with fear. They cried to God in their distress, and then they turned to Moses and began to blame him for bringing them out of Egypt, only to die in the wilderness.

Moses stood forth before them. His fearless courage did not fail, for he was sure that God would not allow His people to be taken back to Egypt and its cruel bondage. In a loud voice he cried to the people, " Fear ye not, stand still, and see the salvation of the Lord, which He will show to you to-day : for the Egyptians whom ye have seen to-day, ye shall see them again no more for ever. The Lord shall fight for you, and ye shall hold your peace."

Then Moses prayed to God, and God answered him, " Wherefore criest thou unto Me ? Speak unto the children of Israel, that they go forward." That seemed a hard saying to these despairing people. They were hemmed in by a high mountain on one side, and bare desert hills on the other. They had the sea in front of them, and the Egyptian host was pressing on behind. The night came on, and in the darkness the people saw the pillar of fire, but it was not seen by the Egyptians. When the morning came, they went forward in great wonder to the Red Sea.

As they came near the shore of the sea, Moses lifted up his rod, and God sent a strong wind that blew the waters of the Red Sea back, until they stood like a wall on either side, and left a dry passage between. The people went down into this passage, and passed through the midst of the sea to the dry land on the other side. The Egyptians followed them down into the midst of the sea, but their heavy chariot wheels sank in the soft wet sand. When they took off the wheels, and lashed their horses to urge them on, they found that they could go no farther. Then the wind ceased, and the Egyptians saw their danger, and they said, " Let us flee from the face of Israel ; for the Lord fighteth for them against the Egyptians."

It was too late. God said to Moses, " Stretch out thine hand over the sea." When Moses stretched out his hand over the sea, the waters came rushing and roaring back again, and Pharaoh and all his host were drowned in the depths of the sea. In the morning the people of Israel saw the Egyptians dead upon the seashore. There remained not so much as one of them alive. But the children of Israel had passed upon dry land to the other side.

When the people saw what God had done, they feared Him with a new heart, and they believed in Him and in His servant Moses. There was great joy among them. Then Moses sang a noble song of praise, and Miriam, his sister, took up the strain, and called on the women to bless God, saying, " Sing ye to the Lord for He hath triumphed gloriously : the horse and his rider hath He thrown into the midst of the sea."

Moses in the Mount

As the children of Israel journeyed on through the wilderness many strange things happened to them. But God watched over them and was patient with them. Sometimes the wells by which they encamped had bitter water, and they were fretful, but God made the waters sweet. Sometimes they were faint with hunger, for their food was scarce, and they longed to be back in Egypt where they had lived with plenty. But God sent the manna, and it fell every morning around them, except on the Sabbath day. Sometimes they were attacked by enemies, but God fought for them and they overcame. Often they grew weary of the desert and its life, and they murmured against God and His ways.

All this was a grief of mind to Moses. He was a brave and a noble leader. He loved the people and sought their good. He had a strong faith in God, and God, when he sought Him in prayer, spoke to him as a man speaks to his friend. God spoke to Moses as He spoke to no other man who ever lived. So God purposed to make known to this discontented and complaining people His wise and holy laws, and this is the story of how He made known His commandments to Moses.

In their wanderings through the desert they came to Mount Sinai. Mount Sinai is near to Horeb, where Moses kept the flock of Jethro, and where he saw the bush that burned with fire. It was a broad plain, but a lonely place, far from any other people. Its bare and rocky hills rose up all around, and the highest of them was this Mount Sinai, which was many thousand feet high. In this quiet and far-off place, Moses told the people to pitch their tents, and to make a camp, for they would stay for many days in this land of Horeb.

One day God called to Moses out of the thick cloud which rested on the top of Mount Sinai. He reminded him of what He had done to the Egyptians, when He had delivered the people from them, and He recalled the kindness with which He had kept them in the desert. He said to him that He was now about to make known His wise and holy laws to the people, that they might keep them. So He told Moses to command the people to bathe themselves, and be clean, and to wash their clothes, and then to wait in silence, for three days, not far from the foot of the mount.

On the morning of the third day God called Moses up to the top of the mount to speak with Him.

God told Moses many wonderful things, so that Moses knew more about God and God's ways than any other man. The people began to be terrified, as they heard the thunderings and saw the mountain quaking, but Moses told them why God had come to them to Mount Sinai.

" Fear not," he said, " for God is come to prove

you, and that His fear may be before your faces, that ye sin not."

Then, because God wanted the people to love Him and to obey Him, He gave Moses what we now know as the Ten Commandments. They begin with the great saying, " I am the Lord thy God, which have brought thee out of the land of Egypt, out of the house of bondage. Thou shalt have no other gods before Me."

Then they tell us how God wants us to be true, and faithful, and gentle, and how we should honour our father and mother, and how we should live with all mindfulness of Him, and with loving kindness to our fellow-men.

We are told that God wrote these Ten Commandments on two tables of stone. They were written in that way that they might not be lost or destroyed. And these Ten Commandments never have been forgotten. Every Hebrew child was taught them in the land of Israel, and every Hebrew child is taught them to this day. Jesus learned them when He was a boy in Nazareth. And when He went about teaching the people, He often told them to keep these commandments which Moses had received from God. For He knew that God gave them to make men wise, and to make them good. No one will come to know God, or to love Him, and no one can serve Him well who will mock at these wise and holy laws given to Moses in the mount.

Over Jordan to the Promised Land

The wilderness journey was over and the children of Israel were ready to enter into the Promised Land. It was called by this name, because it was the land promised to Abraham, and Isaac, and Jacob. All the men and women who had come out of Egypt, except Joshua and Caleb, were dead. But their children had grown up, and they were hardy and brave and skilled in war.

When Moses led the people to the border of the desert they pitched their camp on the slope of a great valley. Through this valley the river Jordan flowed. It rushes swiftly down from the mountains away in the north. The people came in sight of the land across the river, and saw that it was a lovely land, with green pastures and many springs of water.

It is a sad bit of the story that Moses was forbidden to enter the land. But God gave him a view over the whole length of it. He told him to go up to the top of a hill called Pisgah. Moses went up and stood, looking across the river, and saw how beautiful was the home which God had prepared for His people. He never came back. He died, and God buried him in a grave that no one ever knew. Some say that God came, as he was dying, and kissed him.

For thirty days the people mourned for Moses. They had sad faces and heavy hearts, when they became sure that Moses, the servant of the Lord, was dead. Moses had told them who should be their new leader. He had set him before the people, and laid his hands upon him to give him his blessing. His name was Joshua, and he was a man of courage and of faith, like Moses. Joshua was fearful when he was called to this service, so God said to him, "As I was with Moses, so I will be with thee : I will

Through this valley the river Jordan flowed.

not fail thee, nor forsake thee. Be strong, and of a good courage."

Joshua then gathered the people together, and told them that, after three days, they would pass over Jordan. He sent two men across the river to find out the way, and to report upon the land and the people. In the darkness of the night they forded the Jordan, and came to Jericho, and a woman named

O.O.S E

Rahab received them into her house. The king of Jericho heard that these two strange men had come, and he sent men to take them. But Rahab hid them under stalks of flax on the flat roof of her house. She believed God, and she was kind to His people.

When the two spies came back they told Joshua all that had happened to them and what they had seen. They were sure that the land could be taken most easily, and that God would deliver the whole land into their hands. They said that the news of the coming of the people of Israel had been spread far and wide, and they reported, "All the inhabitants of the country do faint because of us."

Next morning Joshua rose up early, and he removed the camp down to the banks of the Jordan.

The first to go down to the very edge of the river were a company of priests. They took the ark of the covenant, shining with gold. It had two angels with outspread wings at both ends. This ark held Aaron's rod, a pot of manna, and the two tables of stone on which the Ten Commandments were engraved. Joshua gave the ark this chief place, because it was sacred to God, and because it told the people that they must depend upon God alone.

The priests were clothed in white garments. They took up the ark upon their shoulders and carried it right down to the brink of the river. The river was in flood and a great stream was sweeping down between the banks. But the priests did not stop for a moment.

As they stepped into the water God opened up a pathway for them. The waters divided and stood up as a heap on both sides, in the same way as the Red Sea had done when they came out of Egypt. The priests went forward with the ark into the middle of the river. Then they stood still and waited. The people from the bank saw this strange sight, and were no longer afraid. They stepped into the river bed, with their children and their flocks and herds, and all passed over in the land of Canaan.

It was a day of great joy to the people, and a day to be kept in remembrance. So twelve men were chosen, one out of each tribe, and they were told to take a large stone out of the river and to carry it to the bank on the Canaan side. They built these stones into a monument, to be a memorial of this passing over Jordan into the land of promise. So that, in the time to come, when the children asked their fathers and mothers, " What mean ye by these stones ? " they could tell them this story of the crossing of the Jordan.

We understand why the people had such gladness. They had entered a lovely and fertile land, a land that flowed, as they said, " with milk and honey." They had begun a new and richer life. But, best of all, they saw that God had fulfilled the promise made to their fathers. They gave a deep reverence to Joshua. " They feared him, as they feared Moses, all the days of his life." Joshua bade them remember God, and told them that this great wonder had been done " that all the people of the earth might know the hand of the Lord, that it is mighty ; that ye might fear the Lord your God for ever."

Joshua, God's Loyal Soldier

Moses was the leader of God's people through the wilderness. Joshua was their leader in the conquest of the land of Canaan. He was a choice young man, for there was no other so loyal and noble as he was. He had been Moses' minister, and that means that he waited upon Moses and did his bidding. Best of all, as we are told, " he departed not out of the tabernacle." He loved to worship God in His House. This was the young man whom God chose to be His good soldier and to drive out the wicked Canaanites who were defiling the land.

There are three stories which can be told to show how loyal a soldier Joshua was. The first of these describes a battle that took place in the wilderness. As the people of Israel were passing on their way, a tribe called the Amalekites came down to stop them. They were wild, fierce, lawless, evil-living robbers, and they thought they could easily attack and defeat the Israelites. They were trained men of war and well armed, and Moses did not feel sure that the people of Israel could withstand them. So he was anxious and troubled in mind.

He called young Joshua and bade him gather a

band of soldiers to go down against the Amalekites.
Moses then went up to a hill from which he saw the
battlefield, for the purpose of watching the battle
and encouraging the people. He sat on a large
stone, and lifted up his hands in prayer to God. As
the day passed on, and the battle continued, his arms
became weary. Then Aaron, his brother, with a
friend called Hur, held up his arms. When his arms
were held up, Joshua and his men prevailed, and in
the evening the Amalekites were beaten, and they
fled away. Joshua had shown that he was a good
soldier of God.

In the second story we are told how Joshua fought
his first battle in the land of Canaan. In that battle
he took the city of Jericho, drove out its people, and
levelled its walls. It was a strong city with high
walls, and the people thought they were secure when
they shut the gates of their city, and looked out upon
the Israelites dwelling in their tents in the plain.
Joshua knew that the swords and spears of the men
of Israel could not prevail against the thick walls of
this city. But he remembered that it was God who
had fought for Israel against Amalek, so he prepared
a plan which trusted entirely in God and His power.

He called the people together and arranged a long
procession which should march round the city. First
in order there came rank after rank of soldiers. Then
there followed seven priests, with trumpets made of
rams' horns. Then there came the sacred ark of
God, with its gleaming angels, and this was carried

on the shoulders of priests clothed in white robes. There followed, behind the ark, a great host of armed men. This procession walked slowly around the walls of Jericho. They kept perfect silence. Not a word was spoken by any one. Only the priests blew with their trumpets, and the walls of Jericho re-echoed with the sound.

This march round the city, in solemn silence, was repeated every day for six days. It was a strange sight to the men of Jericho, and they watched it with wondering eyes from the walls of their city. On the seventh day the procession started early in the morning light, before the sun had risen high. Then they marched round the city seven times. As they were going round for the seventh time, the priests blew loud blasts on the trumpets, and then Joshua cried to the people, " Shout, for the Lord hath given you the city."

Then a wonderful change took place. " When the people heard the sound of the trumpet, and when the people shouted with a great shout, the wall fell down flat so that the people went up into the city, every man straight before him, and they took the city." It was a very wicked city, and God destroyed it. But Joshua remembered Rahab, and he brought her and her kinsfolk out of the city, and saved them alive, because she had hidden the messengers he sent to spy out the land.

The third story of Joshua's warfare had a sad beginning. As the people began to pass up into the land they came to a city on the hillside named Ai. A band of soldiers went up to take it, thinking that it would be an easy prey. But the men of Ai came out and repulsed the Israelites, and slew a number of their men. They came back to Joshua in fear. Joshua was troubled at this defeat, but he felt sure that this was a punishment because of some wrong. He discovered that a man named Achan had taken of the spoils of Jericho which he had been forbidden to take. He had hidden a wedge of gold, and a rich, embroidered garment, in the floor of his tent. That was why God was angry. Joshua punished Achan for his wicked deed. Then he sent another band to take Ai, and God was with them and they took the city. In this way Joshua fought battle after battle, until the whole land was in possession of the children of Israel.

When Joshua had grown old, he began to fear that some of the people of Israel were not keeping God's commandments, and were not loving and serving Him as they should. One day he gathered together all the chief men among the people and he spoke to them most earnestly, and pleaded with them to love and serve God only. He called upon them to renew their covenant to God. He said to them, " Choose you this day whom ye will serve." For he was afraid that they would serve and worship the idols of the heathen. Then he added, "As for me and my house, we will serve the Lord."

The people were greatly moved that day, and they

answered, " God forbid that we should forsake the Lord to serve other gods." So they made the covenant, and set up a great stone under an oak as a witness. So Joshua died in peace, assured that the people would be faithful to God, as he, God's loyal soldier, had been.

The people who heard Joshua speak never forgot that day. His ringing words and his shining face moved them to a new courage. The good men who were round about him kept the vow they had made to him as long as they lived. But when these men died, the people began to forget the covenant they had made, and to follow the custom of their godless neighbours. Then the heathen nations round about them began to oppress them, and to make their lives miserable. The land was filled with strife, and all the hopes and promises which Joshua had taught them to expect were now forgotten. They entered upon dark days of poverty and hardship and fear, because they had lost their faith in God and no longer kept His commandments. God cannot give us His blessing if we will not walk in His ways.

THE DARK DAYS OF THE STORY

THE HEROISM OF GIDEON

THE children of Israel lived in Canaan for a long time in peace. They planted vines and olives and fig trees. Their gardens brought forth delicious fruits, and they tended their cattle on the hills. But they had fierce enemies all around them, who worshipped false gods and made idols. One of the false gods they worshipped was Baal. The people of Israel began to imitate them, and to forget all that God had done for them. Then they became weak and feeble, and their neighbours assailed them, until they cried unto God in their fear, and He delivered them.

One of their most heroic leaders, who were called judges, was Gideon. When he was a young man the Midianites had overcome the people of Israel, and oppressed them. They lived in terror of these fierce foes, and many of them fled into hiding places. Gideon believed in God, and his spirit was stirred when he saw God's people enslaved and despoiled.

One night he was threshing corn in a secret place behind a wine press, so as to hide it from the Midianites. While he was brooding over the wrongs done to his people, an angel appeared to him and said, ' The

Lord is with thee, thou mighty man of valour."
Gideon replied, " Oh, my Lord, if the Lord be with
us, why then is all this befallen us ? "   But God
said to him, " Go in this thy might, and thou shalt
save Israel from the hand of the Midianites : have
not I sent thee ? " Gideon still felt that the task
was too great for him, and God said to him again,
" Surely I will be with thee, and thou shalt smite the
Midianites as one man."   Then God gave him a sign.
Fire came out of a rock, and consumed the offering
which Gideon presented to the angel.   So Gideon built
an altar there and called it by the name of Jehovah-
Shalom, which means, " The Lord send peace."

That same night God gave him his first command.
Gideon's father, Joash, had begun to worship idols,
and had built an altar to Baal.   God told Gideon to
throw down the altar to Baal, and to cut down the
grove of trees around it, and to build another altar,
where he would offer a young bullock in sacrifice to
the God of Israel.   Gideon chose out ten young men
of his father's servants to be his companions in this
daring deed.   They went up to the altar in the night-
time and destroyed it, and built the new altar of
sacrifice to God.   In the morning the worshippers of Baal
saw this new altar and the sacrifice still burning upon it.

In their wonder and anger they asked, " Who hath
done this thing ? " and they were told that young
Gideon had done it.   They called upon Joash to
bring out his son, for he must die.   Joash was not
willing to deliver his son to them, for he knew in his

heart that Baal was not a god at all. So he said scornfully, " Will ye plead for Baal ? If he be a god, let him plead for himself, because one hath cast down his altar."

The Midianites saw that Gideon was putting them to defiance. They gathered their men of war, and the soldiers of some neighbouring tribes, to punish the Israelites and to teach them that they could not, in this way, cast down the altars of Baal. Gideon's courage rose high in this time of danger, and he blew the trumpet to summon all the brave hearts of Israel to war. He sent messengers through all the land, and thirty-two thousand gathered to him, beside a well on the hillside, called the Well of Harod.

But God did not mean to deliver Israel by this host of armed men. He told Gideon to address them, and to tell any of them who were fearful and afraid, to leave the camp and go home. At once twenty-two thousand men, whose hearts had begun to fail them, departed. Again God spoke, and said that even the ten thousand men who were left were too many. So he told Gideon to lead them down to the stream in the valley, that they might satisfy their thirst. The most of the men kneeled down at the edge of the water, and drank greedily of the stream. But three hundred drank only by taking up the water in their hands, and so they lapped the water, slowly in the way that a dog drinks. In this way the three hundred showed their self-control, and God said that they were enough.

That night these three hundred waited and watched.

Gideon, along with his servant, stole down in the darkness to the camp of the Midianites. Outside one of the tents they heard two men speaking. One of them told his dream. "Behold, I dreamed a dream, and, lo, a cake of barley bread tumbled into the host of Midian, and came unto a tent, and smote it, that it fell, and overturned it." The other answered with fear in his eyes, "This is nothing else save the sword of Gideon; into his hand hath God delivered Midian, and all the host." Gideon returned, thanking God for this message from strange lips.

He divided his men into three companies. To each of them he gave a trumpet, held in one hand, and an empty earthen pitcher, held in the other. Into the pitcher he put a lighted torch, whose flame was hidden by the pitcher. Then he said that he would blow with a trumpet, and proclaim, "The sword of the Lord and of Gideon," and then they would break the pitchers and flare the torches. So the three hundred men went down to surround the camp, and they blew the trumpets, brake the pitchers, waved the torches in their hands, and cried, as Gideon directed. The Midianites thought that a great host was upon them, and in the darkness began to strike with their swords against their fellows, until all the host ran with shouts of fear, fleeing out of danger. Gideon and his men pursued them, and as God promised, a great victory was given to Israel.

Jephthah and His Daughter

We wonder why the people of Israel, after all that God had done for them, and after such a victory and deliverance had been given them through Gideon, could ever forget God and His kindness. But they were always being tempted to be like their neighbours, and to worship the gods of the heathen, and then God delivered them into the hands of their enemies. So it came to pass that the children of Ammon crossed over the Jabbok to fight against the Israelites who lived in the land of Gilead. They were a fierce and war-like tribe, and the people of Gilead in their misery sought God's help and power.

There was a man named Jephthah who belonged to Gilead. He was a brave soldier and a true man, who loved his country and trusted in God. But his family cherished an ill-will against him, and they scorned him because of his birth, and openly mocked him. The men of Gilead took part with the family, and were unkind to him, and drove him out of the city. He found a home in the mountains, and gathered a band of lawless and desperate men, to whom he was chief and captain. The whole land knew of the valour of Jephthah's band.

When the news came that the king of Ammon was marching against Gilead, the leading men of the city went up to Jephthah's stronghold, to ask him to come to their help. He looked at them in silence, and then said, " Did not ye hate me, and expel me out of my father's house ? Why are ye come unto me now when ye are in distress ? " The elders of Gilead confessed their need of him, and said to him. " Go with us, and be our head over all the inhabitants of Gilead." Jephthah could not trust these men, who had used him so unkindly, and he said, " If ye bring me home again to fight against the children of Ammon, and the Lord deliver them before me, shall I be your head ? " And the men of Gilead took an oath that they would make him head and captain over them, and they said, " The Lord be witness between us." Then Jephthah went into God's presence, and poured out his heart in prayer.

He began his defence of Gilead by sending messengers to the king of Ammon to ask him what he was doing in the land of Gilead, and why he had come to fight with the people. The king of Ammon said that the land of Gilead belonged to the Ammonites.

Jephthah replied that the land had never belonged to the Ammonites. It had been in possession of the Amorites, who were a most evil-minded and wicked tribe, and that under God's will the children of Israel had taken it from them. Then he said that it was God who in former days had dispossessed the Amorites, and that the land could not be given now to worshippers of idols like the Ammonites. He asked the king of Ammon, " Wilt not thou possess that which Chemosh, thy god, giveth thee to possess ? " Chemosh was the god worshipped by the king of Ammon, and

Jephthah meant to say that he was no god at all. The God of Israel, Jephthah said, He would judge between the children of Israel and the children of Ammon.

The King of Ammon would not give heed to Jephthah's appeal. Then the Spirit of the Lord came upon Jephthah, and he gathered his men and passed over to fight with the men of Ammon. Before he crossed the river he vowed a vow unto the Lord. " If thou shalt, without fail, deliver the children of Israel into mine hands, then it shall be that whatsoever cometh forth of the doors of my house to meet me, when I return in peace from the children of Ammon, shall surely be the Lord's, and I will offer it up for a burnt offering." Jephthah went on to fight with the Ammonites, and the Lord delivered them into his hands. He took their cities and overcame the people.

Now Jephthah had a daughter whom he deeply loved. She was his only child ; beside her, he had neither son nor daughter. When she was left behind in Gilead, she waited with anxious heart for some message from her father. She knew how strong and fierce were the men of Ammon, but she knew that Jephthah fought for the God of Israel, and that God would help him. The tidings of the great victory Jephthah had won, reached Gilead before Jephthah and his men returned. Jephthah's daughter took her timbrels, and sped out to meet her father, as he was drawing near to the city of Gilead. She made the timbrels ring and chime, and she danced in her joyous delight. When Jephthah saw her coming, he stood still in his horror. He was stricken into a grief he could not control. He remembered his vow, and he was cast down into deep sorrow, that his beloved daughter was the first to come forth out of the doors of his house to meet him.

As she drew near, he rent his clothes and said to her, "Alas, my daughter! Thou hast brought me very low, for I have opened my mouth unto the Lord, and I cannot go back." It was an awful moment, Jephthah's daughter was young, with all her days before her. Her hopes were high, and her heart had been filled with joy. In a moment all was clouded in darkness. But she was a girl of a noble spirit, and she knew that a vow made to God must not be broken. So in a low, quiet voice she said, " My father, if thou hast opened thy mouth unto the Lord, do to me according to that which hath proceeded out of thy mouth."

Jephthah, like his daughter, knew that his solemn oath must be kept. He was grateful to God for His mercy to Gilead. So when his daughter said, " Let this thing be done for me : let me alone two months." Jephthah said to her, " Go." She took with her her companions, and for two months, amidst the silence of the hills, she mourned over her sad fate. Then she came back to her father that he might keep his vow. He did not offer her as he would have offered a lamb on the altar. But she went to live her life in loneliness. She had no home, and no little children to love and care for. She was consecrated to a lifetime of silence. Once a year, in aftertimes, the maidens of Israel went up to the mountains to spend four days in lamenting the heroic daughter of Jephthah.

SAMSON'S SUPREME SACRIFICE

In the dark days of the history, when the judges ruled, there was a man whose name was Manoah, and he had no child. But an angel came to his wife, and said that God would give them a son. The angel said that this child, who was to be born, would be one who should deliver Israel and the land from their enemies. One strange thing the angel added. That was that the boy must not drink wine, nor eat grapes, and that his hair must never be cut. By this the angel meant that from his infancy the boy should be marked as one who was set apart to serve God. So the child was born, and they called his name Samson, and he grew strong, and the Lord blessed him.

At this time the people of Israel were being troubled by the Philistines. They lived in the broad plain down at the sea, and they had strong cities, beautiful temples, and richly furnished houses. The people of Israel had been forgetting God again, and the Philistines were pressing in upon them, and subduing their land. Samson had been sent by God so that, when he became a man, he might deliver Israel out of the hands of the Philistines.

He grew up a great, strong-limbed, sunny-faced, brave-hearted young man. He had a joyous spirit and a frank manner, and he loved to do many strange things in his reckless courage. He was the strongest man of whom we read, and many of his feats of strength were impossib'e to any other one.

One day he went down into the vineyard country of the Philistines. A young lion came roaring against him. Samson seized him as he would a kid of the flocks, with nothing but his hands, and tore him in pieces. The Philistines began to watch this strong man and lay plots against him. At another time Samson caught three hundred foxes, tied firebrands to their tails, and let them go into the ripening corn of the Philistines, which was ready for the harvest. It was set on fire and burned up, with the olive trees and vineyards that were near it. On another day he went down to Gaza, which is a Philistine city. The men of Gaza surrounded the house all night, intending to kill him in the morning. Samson rose at midnight, and took the two great doors of the city gate, and the two posts on which they hung, and carried them to the top of a hill before Hebron.

Now if Samson had been as wise as he was strong, and if he had always kept God's commandments as faithfully as his father and mother had taught him, he would have been a great leader of Israel, and lived out his days in full honour. But he liked to please himself, and too often he did things of which it is a shame to speak. The Philistines had marked him as a dangerous enemy, and they saw in his bold and reckless habits their chance of ensnaring him and putting him to death.

He grew very fond of a woman of the Philistines whose name was Delilah, and he often paid her a visit. The lords of the Philistines went to her and promised her eleven hundred pieces of silver if she would find out the secret of that great strength which had put them in fear. "Entice him," they said, " and see wherein his great strength lieth, and by what means we may prevail against him."

Delilah began by asking him wherein his strength lay, and how she might bind him so that he could not set himself free. Samson said that she was to bind him with seven green withs, that were never dried. There were men lying in wait in her house. So she bound him, and she cried, " The Philistines be upon thee, Samson." She intended that these men would burst in upon him, and take him when he was bound. Samson brake the withs as easily as a thread of tow breaks at a touch of fire.

Delilah mocked him, and said to him that he had told her lies. So he said that she should bind him with new ropes, that had never been used. She did so, and again cried, " The Philistines be upon thee, Samson." He broke the ropes as though they had been threads. Once more she reproached him, and this time he said that she should weave the seven locks of his head with the web, and fasten them to the pin of the beam. Samson slept as she wove, and

when she cried, " The Philistines be upon thee," he
rose up and went away, with the web hanging to the
pin of the weaving beam.

Now Delilah broke out in reproach. " How canst
thou say, I love thee, when thine heart is not with
me ? Thou hast mocked me these three times."
Then Samson told her his secret. " There hath not
come a razor upon mine head ; if I be shaven my
strength will go from me, and I shall become weak,
and be like any other man." Delilah saw that he had
told her all his heart. She called for the lords of the
Philistines, and they came, with the money they
promised her, in their hand. She made Samson sleep,
and while he slept, she called a man who shaved off
the great locks of his hair. Then she cried, " The
Philistines be upon thee, Samson." Samson awoke,
and thought to shake himself, and find his strength
as before. " He wist not that the Lord was departed
from him." He had sinned wilfully, broken his
vow, and God gave him over to the hands of the
Philistines.

They took him, put out his eyes, bound him with
fetters of brass, and made him grind like a slave in
the prison house. What a sight it must have been
to see this man, once so strong, so bright, and so
eager, and once dedicated to God, now a poor, enslaved, blind man. But the locks of his hair began
to grow, and his strength began to return. When the
lords of the Philistines appointed a day to offer a
sacrifice of thanksgiving unto Dagon, their god, for

they thought that their god had delivered Samson into their hands, they sent for Samson to make them sport, and he performed his feats of strength. Then they set him between the two pillars which upheld their temple. Samson asked the young lad who guided him to let him feel the two pillars, that he might lean upon them. The house was full of men and women, and the lords of the Philistines were there, so that about three thousand looked on from the high galleries, when Samson was making sport before them. Samson's heart was heavy and his shame was deep, for he saw how foolish, and wilful, and wasteful, his life had been.

He took hold of the two pillars, and he prayed, " O Lord God, remember me, I pray thee, only this once, O God, that I may be at once avenged on the Philistines for my two eyes." Then he said, " Let me die with the Philistines." He bowed himself, putting forth all his strength, and as he pulled down the pillars, the house fell upon the Philistines, and thousands were buried among its ruins. " The dead which he slew at his death were more than they which he slew in his life." That was Samson's supreme sacrifice.

RUTH AMONG THE EARS OF CORN

There lived during the time of the judges in the little town of Bethlehem a man named Elimelech. He had a pleasant home, which was his own possession, with fertile fields around it. But a long drought fell upon the land, and the harvest failed. In the dreadful famine that followed, many were almost starving. Across the Jordan, in the land of Moab, there was an abundance of food. So Elimelech and his wife Naomi and their two boys left Bethlehem to live in the land of Moab.

But many troubles befell the little Hebrew family. Elimelech died, and Naomi learned how hard and how lonely is a widow's lot. But she made friends among the Moabites, and they were kind to her in her sorrow. Her two sons grew up, and both of them married Moabitish women. The name of one of them was Orpah, and of the other, Ruth. They had a very short time of happiness, for both Naomi's sons fell sick and died. So Naomi and her two daughters-in-law were left desolate.

These sore trials and bereavements cast Naomi into gloom. She began to wonder if her husband had done right in leaving the land of Canaan, in which God had given them an inheritance, and had promised them a blessing. The Moabites were heathen, and worshipped the god Chemosh. Naomi knew that she could find her safety and her peace only under the care of the God of Israel. At that time some travellers brought news of a wonderful harvest in the land of Canaan. The barns were stored with corn, and there was abundance of bread. Naomi made up her mind to go back to Bethlehem.

Now Naomi had often spoken to her daughters-in-law, Orpah and Ruth, about the God of Israel,

and His love and care for His people. They had seen
how true and how kind she was, and how gently and
lovingly she had dealt with them. They also began
to put their trust in the God of Israel. So when
Naomi told them that she was going back to the land
of Canaan, they said that they would go with her,
and they set out on the road to Bethlehem.

But they had gone only a little way when Naomi
stopped, and said to her two companions, " Go,
return, each to her mother's house." She knew
they might be looked upon with scornful eyes, and
given no welcome by the people of Bethlehem. So
she kissed them and bade them farewell. But they
said to her, " Surely we will return with thee unto
thy people," and, as they spoke, their sobs broke
forth, and they wept many tears. But Naomi per-
sisted, and said, " Turn again, my daughters, go your
way ; it grieveth me much for your sakes that the
hand of the Lord is gone out against me." Then
Orpah, although with tears, kissed her mother-in-law
and turned back to Moab.

Ruth clung to Naomi. She loved her with a true
affection, and she had learned from Naomi to put her
trust in the God of Israel. Then Naomi said to her,
" Thy sister-in-law is gone back unto her people and
unto her gods ; return thou after thy sister-in-law."
Ruth broke out in a moving appeal. " Entreat me
not to leave thee, or to return from following after
thee : for whither thou goest, I will go : where thou
lodgest, I will lodge : thy people shall be my people,

and thy God my God. Where thou diest will I die, and there will I be buried: the Lord do so to me, and more also, if aught but death part thee and me." Naomi looked at her with grateful eyes, and when she saw her steadfast mind, she took her hand, and they set out together on the road to Bethlehem.

When they came to the gate of Bethlehem, and passed through it, the people stood still to look at them. Some in Bethlehem had heard that Naomi had been bereaved, and others may have known of her sorrow and care. She had gone out in the flush of youth and health. Now she was old and gray-haired and worn, as well as weary with her journey. When they saw her, they pitied her and said, " Is this Naomi ? " Then Naomi said, " Call me not Naomi (which means pleasant), call me Mara (which means bitter), for the Lord hath dealt very bitterly with me."

Naomi and Ruth came to Bethlehem at the beginning of the barley harvest. They were in great poverty. So Ruth said to Naomi that she would go out with the poor women, who gleaned in the fields after the reapers, to pick up any of the ears which they had dropped. Naomi did not feel happy that Ruth should go out and glean in the fields, but she gave her consent because they were in such sore need. So Ruth went out timidly, feeling herself to be a stranger in a strange land. She came to the field of a kind and courteous man named Boaz. He saw her to be a stranger, and he asked who she was. He

had noticed that she was sweet and comely in appear-
ance, and modest in her bearing. He asked his
overseer, " Whose damsel is this ? " He was told
that she was Ruth, the Moabitish damsel, that had
come out of that country along with Naomi. Boaz
had heard of the coming of Ruth, and of her kindness
to Naomi. He had been told that she had put her
faith in the God of Israel, so he said to her, " The
Lord recompense thy work, and a full reward be given
thee of the Lord God of Israel, under whose wings
thou art come to trust."

Now as Boaz saw Ruth day by day, he began to
love her, and he made up his mind to make her his
wife. He learned that although Naomi and Ruth
were so poor, there was a piece of land in Bethlehem
which had once belonged to them. Elimelech had
sold it, when he went to live in Moab. Naomi knew
of this land, but she was too poor to buy it back.
Boaz went to the elders of the city, as they sat in the
gate, which was the place where they carried on the
affairs of the city. He told them that he was about
to make Ruth his wife, and he wanted to buy back
the inheritance which should have been hers. By
this time Ruth had become well known and tenderly
beloved by all the people of Bethlehem, and they
rejoiced in what Boaz had done. So Ruth became
the wife of Boaz, who had been so kind to her and to
Naomi in their time of need, and no one was more
gladdened in heart at all the tokens of the goodness
of God than Naomi, who loved her all her days.

HANNAH, THE MOTHER OF SAMUEL

The dark days of Israel's history had not yet passed away, but a better time was coming. In the days that were to come the people of Israel would return, in a new faith, to God and to His service. This story of Hannah, the mother of Samuel, tells us how that better time began.

Hannah was the wife of Elkanah, who lived to the north of Jerusalem at Mount Ephraim. He had two wives, but he loved Hannah with a very tender affection, and he showed his love by many kindnesses. Hannah had a great sorrow, because she had no children. Sometimes she had to bear cruel reproaches and scornful taunts because she was childless, and in the night-time she wept bitter tears.

Elkanah was a devout man, who taught his household to fear God, and to keep all His commandments. Every year at the due season, he took his family up to Shiloh to attend the solemn feasts observed by the Hebrew people.

Hannah loved to go to this yearly feast at Shiloh, but she was always sadder there than anywhere else. It was when she took part in the solemn services that she felt her sorrow at having no son to give to God's service. Her vexation of heart at one of the feasts, because she was so mocked and scorned, was almost more than she could bear. When her husband Elkanah showed her by his gifts how much he loved her, she

could not eat of the portion, but only wept. Then
Elkanah said, " Hannah, why weepest thou ? And
why eatest thou not ? And why is thy heart grieved ?
Am not I better to thee than ten sons ? " Hannah
rose up from the table, and went into the temple in
bitterness of soul, and prayed unto the Lord, and as
she prayed, she wept.

In her prayers she vowed a vow, and she said, " O
Lord God of Hosts, if Thou wilt indeed look on the
affliction of Thine handmaid, and remember me,
and not forget Thine handmaid, but will give unto
Thine handmaid a man child, then I will give him
unto the Lord all the days of his life."

Now the name of the priest who had charge of the
temple was Eli. He was a good and well-meaning
man, but he was not always wise and watchful. He
was sitting on his seat, and he saw Hannah come in
and kneel down in prayer. But as she prayed, and
made her solemn vow, she did not speak any word
that any one could hear. Only her lips moved, and
Eli marked the opening of her mouth. He called out
in angry rebuke, " How long wilt thou be drunken ?
Put away thy wine from thee." Hannah answered,
" No, my lord, I am a woman of a sorrowful spirit ; I
have drunk neither wine nor strong drink, but have
poured out my soul before the Lord." Eli was vexed
with himself at having misunderstood Hannah, and
he said, " Go in peace : and the God of Israel grant
thee thy petition that thou hast asked of Him."
Then Hannah bowed down and said, " Let thine

handmaid find grace in thy sight." She went out of the temple, with a glad heart and a shining face.

God answered Hannah's prayer, and a little son was given to her. She called him by the name of Samuel, which means ." asked of God," because he had been given to her in answer to her prayer. When Elkanah went back to offer the sacrifices at Shiloh, Hannah did not go with him, for she stayed at home to care for her boy. For over three years she nourished him, and taught him, and trained him. Then, when she thought he was old enough to be presented to God, she went up to Shiloh. When she came to Shiloh she went into the temple leading her little boy by the hand. Then she made her sacrifice of thanks-giving, and came to Eli, and gave the boy into his care.

Eli had thought little or nothing about the woman whom he had seen praying in the silence of the temple. So she said to him, " Oh, my lord, as thy soul liveth, my lord, I am the woman that stood by thee here praying unto the Lord. For this child I prayed : and the Lord hath given me my petition which I have asked of Him. Therefore also I have lent him to the Lord ; as long as he liveth, he shall be lent to the Lord." Then Hannah broke out in a great song of thanksgiving, and said, " My heart rejoiceth in the Lord."

That was Samuel's first sight of the temple, and he could never have forgotten his mother's rapture and joy. She left him behind her with Eli, young as he

was. But every year she sent him some remembrance of her love and care, and Samuel all his life
knew that his mother had given him to the Lord.

THE CHILD IN THE TEMPLE

Eli, the priest in the temple at Shiloh, began to
grow old. His eyes were dim, so that he could not
see. Hannah's little son was growing older, and the
boy became dearly beloved by Eli as he waited on
him, ran his errands, and did his bidding. Eli had
two sons of his own, but they lived evil lives, and did
many wicked deeds. For Eli, although he was a
good man, had not corrected them. So Eli found a
deep joy in the child Samuel. He knew that his
mother had told Samuel all the story of her prayer for
him, and the reason why she had given him that name.
He saw that God had accepted the gift Hannah had
offered, and that Samuel would grow up to serve
God as long as he lived. Although he came to the
temple a very young child, he had been taught to
pray night and morning, and had been trained to be
true and pure. Now, as he lived in the temple, and
waited on Eli, he had come to think of God's house
as his home.

One night Samuel lay down to sleep in the temple.
There was a lamp hung in the temple which was lighted
at the evening hour, and burned all night until the
morning came. In that night Samuel slept on without

a break. But at the darkest hour of the night, just before the dawn, Samuel heard a voice calling him, " Samuel, Samuel."

He was all alone in the temple. The darkness was deep except where the lamp of God was hung. The voice awoke Samuel, and he thought it was the voice of Eli. At once he rose and ran in to Eli and said, " Here am I; for thou calledst me." But Eli said that he had not called him, and he bade him go and lie down again. Samuel wondered who had called him, but he went back and lay down again.

As he lay, the voice called again, " Samuel." Samuel thought that it must be Eli who was calling him, and again he went to him and said, " Here am I, for thou didst call me." We are told that Samuel did not yet know the Lord, neither was the word of the Lord yet revealed unto him. That means that although a boy or girl may know much about God, and have been taught to read His word, and even to understand how great and high and holy God is, they do not know how God speaks to them, and how very near God may come to them. Samuel did not dream that God would actually speak to him, and so he thought it must be the voice of Eli.

Now that is one of the most beautiful things in the story. Eli's voice was the kindest voice that ever fell on Samuel's ears. He was the best man whom Samuel knew. So he thought that when God spoke, He would speak as softly and tenderly and lovingly as Eli spoke. Samuel may have known that God

had sometimes spoken with a voice that made the
mountains quake, and sometimes with angry words
which made men fear. But now his thought was that
when God spoke to him He would speak as Eli spoke.

So when God called Samuel the third time, and
he arose from his bed and went again to Eli and
told him, Eli began to see that it was God who had
called the child. He said to Samuel, " Go, lie down ;
and it shall be if He call thee that thou shalt say,
Speak, Lord : for Thy servant heareth." So Samuel
went and lay down in his place. He had not long to
wait. Through the darkness and in the silence, God
came and called as before, " Samuel, Samuel." Then
Samuel answered, " Speak, for Thy servant heareth."
From that hour Samuel knew the Lord.

The message which God gave to Samuel was one
terrifying in its judgment. As God said to Samuel
it was a message " at which both the ears of every
one that heareth it shall tingle." God told Samuel
that because Eli's sons had made themselves accursed,
and he had not restrained them, He would punish
Eli's house and would bring a stern judgment on his
sons. Their iniquity was so great and so wilful that
it would not be forgiven.

Samuel lay wakeful and wondering until the morning. Then he arose and opened the doors of the
temple, and began to prepare the house of the Lord
for worship. But he did not go near Eli, and he was
afraid to tell Eli what God had showed him. But Eli
had also spent a sleepless night, and he called Samuel

and he asked him, " What is the thing that the Lord hath said unto thee ? I pray thee hide it not from me. God do so to thee, and more also, if thou hide anything from me of all the things that He said unto thee."

It was a hard thing for Samuel to tell Eli what God had said should be done to Eli's sons. But he had been brought up to be a boy who should speak the truth, and he told Eli every whit and hid nothing from him. Eli sat for a while in silence, and then lifting up his blind eyes, he softly said, " It is the Lord ; let Him do what seemeth Him good." He knew that his two sons, whose names were Hophni and Phinehas, deserved the punishment of God.

After that night the people saw a change in Samuel. They saw that God had spoken to him, and the whole land knew that he was a prophet of God, and that he knew the mind and the will of the Lord.

THE EARLY YEARS OF THE KINGDOM

The Crowning of King Saul

WHEN Samuel, the prophet and judge, had grown old, some of the men of Israel came to him to ask him to get them a king. The king they wanted was a daring and gallant soldier, who would defend them from their enemies. Samuel was vexed at this request, for it seemed to him that they were forgetting that God was their King, and were becoming like the heathen nations around them. So he went into his chamber, and prayed to God, and God told him to grant the people their desire.

Now there was a young man of the tribe of Benjamin whose name was Saul. He was a fine looking youth, very tall, and when he walked he held himself like a soldier. There was not another like him in all Israel. He was a wise young man, and modest in his speech, and he lived a life of purity, and served his father with loyalty.

One morning when Saul's father, who was a man of wealth, arose, he found that his asses had gone astray. He told Saul to take one of the servants and search for them. The two men travelled far and wide, over hill and dale, but could not find them. As they went through the land they came to Ramah, where Samuel lived. At the foot of the hill, on which the little city was built, Saul's servant proposed that they should consult Samuel, the prophet, for he might be able to tell them about the asses. They climbed up the steep road, and as they were passing through the gate Samuel came out. As soon as Samuel saw young Saul, God said to him, "Behold the man whom I spake to thee of! this same shall reign over my people."

Samuel took him into his house, and prepared a feast, and set Saul in the chief place at the table as the guest of honour. In the evening, when the air was cool, he took Saul up to the flat roof of the house, where people used to sit. He began to speak to him tenderly of God, and of God's ways, and of His love and care for Israel, and of His great promises made to Abraham and to Isaac and to Jacob and to Moses, in times gone by.

On the next morning, as soon as the sun was up, he called Saul and he told him that he would accompany him a part of the way. As they went down the hill he bade Saul's servant pass on before, for he wanted to speak to Saul alone. When they came to a quiet place, and no one was in sight, he took a vial of oil and poured the oil on Saul's head. In the East it was the usual way to honour a friend by anointing the head with oil. So Mary of Bethany broke her box of precious ointment over the head of Jesus. And it was the way in which they always honoured the king. After he had poured the oil on Saul's head, he kissed him, and he explained what this anointing meant by saying, " Is it not because the Lord hath anointed thee to be captain over His inheritance ? "

Samuel lost no time in calling all the people together. When all the tribes were gathered at Mizpeh he told them that they must now choose a king. First, they chose the tribe of Benjamin. Then they chose the family of Kish, Saul's father. Then they chose Saul. Saul had come up to this great assembly, but when he found himself chosen to be king he was overcome, and in his shyness he went and hid himself. But they found him, and brought him out before Samuel. They all marked his great height, for he was higher than any of the people from his shoulders and upward. Then Samuel said to all the people, " See ye him whom the Lord hath chosen, that there is none like him among all the people ! " Then all the people gave a great shout and cried, " God save the king."

As Saul left the eager and excited assembly, some of the men, who loved and served God, and were glad at heart because God had given them a king, went home with him all the way. But others, who were mean of spirit, despised him, and spoke with contempt, and said, " Can this man save us ? " Saul had looked every inch a king. But he soon gave proof of his call to rule, and his power to defend the people from their enemies. The little city of Jabesh-Gilead, away across the Jordan, was threatened by the king of the Ammonites. They sent messengers to Saul and besought his help. The people felt so distressed at the tidings that they broke out into weeping. Saul heard the weeping as he came out of the field, and, when he was told the reason of it, the Spirit of God came upon him, and his anger was kindled. He summoned all the fighting men of Israel at once, marched across Jordan, and in the early morning they fell upon the Ammonites, and slew some and scattered all the others over the mountains.

When Saul came back the people exulted. They were about to put to death the men who had scorned Saul, and said, " Shall Saul reign over us ? " But Saul was too wise to allow them to do such a deed. Then they all took him to Gilgal, and they crowned him as king, and the whole land rejoiced greatly. It was a splendid beginning ; but the end of Saul's story is strangely sad.

David and Goliath

During all King Saul's reign over Israel the people were attacked and despoiled by the Philistines. The war against them, in which the Israelites defended their homes and their pastures, lasted many years. Saul gathered a great host to drive the Philistines down from the hills to their own sea-coast plain, and soldiers from all parts of the land were to be found in his camp.

Three of these soldiers were the sons of Jesse, a sheep-farmer who kept his flocks in the fields round Bethlehem. Jesse had eight sons, and his youngest son was David. He was an eager, bright-eyed boy. He was fond of music, and could play upon the harp. But he was also strong and active and daring, and his father had set him to watch the flocks, even where wild beasts came down from the hills to devour them. His brave young spirit was vexed at being kept at

His father had set him to watch the flocks.

home, for he was eager to fight with the foes of the people of God.

David's father began to weary for news from his three sons, and he grew anxious to know how they were getting on. He told David to take a little sack of parched corn, and some loaves of bread for his brothers, and he gave him ten cheeses as a present for the captain of their troop. So David rose early in the morning, and set off to the camp of the Israelites.

He came to the camp where the two armies were facing each other, and shouting with loud cries of defiance as they were preparing to meet in battle. He gave the gifts his father had sent to the keeper of the stores, and ran swiftly forward to the ranks of the armed men, and he found his brothers and hailed them.

As he was speaking with his brothers and giving them news of home, and asking eager questions about the war, one of the Philistines, who was a huge giant, named Goliath, came out of the Philistine camp, and proclaimed himself their champion. He shouted across the valley a challenge to any one of the men of Israel to come out and fight with him. He had shown himself, and had boastfully uttered his defiance every day, and cried, " I defy the armies of Israel this day ; give me a man, that we may fight together."

He had a helmet of shining brass on his head, and a coat of gleaming mail to cover him, and a spear with a great thick shaft and a heavy iron head. He had a shield which he wore in the battle, but, as he came striding out of the host, a man walked before him bearing it. As this armed giant came out day by day, Saul and all the men of Israel were greatly afraid when they heard his words. They had no man who would dare to go out and do battle with the Philistine giant.

David stood and listened to his scornful speech. He felt no fear, although he was but a stripling. He asked, " Who is this Philistine that he should defy the armies of the living God ? " When Saul sent for him, David said, " Let no man's heart fail because of him : thy servant will go out and fight this Philistine." Saul looked at David, and said, as he saw how young he was, " Thou art not able to go against this Philistine : for thou art but a youth." But David told him that he had slain a lion and a bear when they had taken a lamb out of the flock, and that God would deliver him out of the hand of the Philistine who had defied the armies of the living God, as He had delivered him from the paw of the lion and the bear. Then Saul said, " Go, and the Lord be with thee."

Saul armed David with his own armour, and put upon him a helmet of brass and a coat of mail, but David found that he could not fight with such armour, and with a strong man's sword. He went down to the brook, chose five smooth stones, put them into his shepherd's bag and took his sling, which he had often used, in his hand. When the Philistine saw this slight, fair-skinned youth coming out to meet him he mocked, and cried, "Am I a dog, that thou comest to me with staves ? "

David said, " Thou comest to me with a sword, and with a spear, and with a shield : but I come to thee in the name of the Lord of Hosts, the God of the armies of Israel, whom thou hast defied : for the battle is the Lord's and He will give you into our hands." Then the Philistine began to go forward to meet David, and David hastened his steps and ran to meet him. He put his hand into his bag and took out a stone, and aiming with great care, he slung the stone and it smote the Philistine in his forehead, and he fell down stunned upon the earth. Then David ran forward, and took the sword of the Philistine and slew him, and cut off his head.

David came back to Saul with Goliath's head in his hands. Saul asked Abner, his chief captain, " Whose son is this youth ? " and Abner said, "As thy soul liveth, O king, I cannot tell." Then Saul asked David himself, and he said, " I am the son of thy servant Jesse the Bethlehemite." Saul was proud of the young man and made him one of his own captains. So David entered the service of the king, and resolved to be true to him and to the God of Israel, whom he loved and served.

DAVID AND JONATHAN

King Saul had a son named Jonathan. He was a sunny-tempered, kindly-natured boy, and he grew up to be a strong and active man of fearless daring and generous spirit. He ran so swiftly, and moved with such grace, that he was called the Gazelle. Saul was proud of his noble son, and all the people of Israel loved him. He was so frank and so full of high spirit that the soldiers of Saul's army would have laid down their lives for him.

There was one deed of his younger days which showed how daring was his courage, and how eager he was to serve his country. The Philistines had made a fort on a hill with a steep cliff on the one side and a steep cliff on the other, and the garrison was placed between the two. Jonathan said to his armour-bearer, who was his friend and companion—"Come, let us go over unto the garrison of the Philistines ; it may be that the Lord will work for us : for there is no restraint to the Lord to save by many or by few." The armour-bearer said, " Behold I am with thee according to thy heart."

As Jonathan and his armour-bearer drew near to the fort, the Philistines saw them, and said to mock them, " Behold the Hebrews come forth out of the holes where they had hid themselves." Then they bade Jonathan and his armour-bearer come up, if they dared. So they climbed up the steep rock with hands and feet, entered the fort, and slew the men of the garrison. When Jonathan came back the men of Israel were glad that Saul had such a son who would afterwards be their king.

Now on that day when David slew Goliath, and Saul was speaking to David his words of thanks, and enlisting him in his service, Jonathan stood by his father's side. He had seen how boldly, and with what trust in God, young David had faced the Philistine. He marked how modestly David spoke. His whole heart went out to him. As we are told, " The soul of Jonathan was knit to the soul of David, and Jonathan loved him as his own soul." He had found a friend who was after his own heart. David wore only the shepherd's coat, but Jonathan stripped himself of his princely robe, and gave David his sword, and his bow, and his girdle. That day the two young men made a covenant of friendship, and they kept their covenant all their days.

When Saul chose David to be one of his captains, he gave him the chance of showing how splendid a soldier he could be. He went out at the head of his troop of men against the Philistines and soon they were driven back from the borders of Israel, and no longer dared to come up and steal the sheep and carry away the corn. After one great battle, where Saul went out with the men of Israel and David was with him, the women of all the cities of Israel came out singing and dancing, with tabrets and other instruments of music to show their joy. As they sang, they chanted these words, " Saul hath slain his thousands and David his ten thousands." Saul was angry that the women of Israel should give David more praise than they gave him. He began to see that the people had become proud of young David, and that they might make him the king, and Jonathan would never wear the crown. So he looked at David with jealous and angry eyes, and began to hate him.

Jonathan was deeply vexed at Saul's anger at David. That anger soon was clearly shown. One day, in a dark and evil mood, Saul sent for David to play upon the harp which David, who was fond of music, played with skill. Saul sat to listen with a javelin in his hand. As he looked at David his anger rose, and he flung the javelin to kill him. David stepped swiftly aside, and went out of Saul's presence. He knew that Saul would try to kill him, and his friend Jonathan was cast into deep sadness because of his father's evil purpose.

So one day Jonathan pleaded with his father. He reminded him that David had not done him any wrong. He recalled his great deed, when he slew Goliath, and he said to Saul, " Thou sawest it, and didst rejoice : wherefore then wilt thou sin against innocent blood to slay David without a cause ? " Saul was ashamed, and promised to Jonathan that he would not seek David's life. Jonathan brought back David to Saul, and David became one of his captains as before.

But an evil spirit began to rule Saul's heart. Again and again Saul tried to put David to death. He began to hunt after him with a band of men. So David became an outlaw, and fled to the mountains, and lived sometimes in the caves and sometimes in the forests. Soon a company of reckless men gathered round about David and protected him. Jonathan saw that he could no longer keep the company of David, deeply as he loved him. He went down into one of David's hiding-places, and when they met they kissed each other, and wept over their sorrow. When they parted, Jonathan said to David, " Go in peace, for as much as we have sworn both of us in the name of the Lord." And Jonathan told David to be strong, because he could be sure that God would help him, and that in time to come he would be king over Israel, and Jonathan would serve him.

The two friends never met again. Jonathan was loyal to his father to the end, and he was slain when he followed him to war on Mount Gilboa. A messenger ran out of the camp, with torn garments and earth on his head, to tell David. David was stricken with grief at the sad tidings. He rent his clothes, and took no food all that day. As he lamented his friend, he sang a noble song, which the world will never forget. " I am distressed for thee, my brother Jonathan : very pleasant hast thou been unto me : thy love to me was wonderful, passing the love of women." There has been no nobler friendship in the world than this friendship of David and Jonathan.

DAVID, THE MAN AFTER GOD'S OWN HEART

After the years of his troubled youth were over David became the king of all Israel. He drove out their enemies, and he built Jerusalem, and made it a strong city. He sang great songs of praise to God in the Holy Place. Sometimes he committed strange sins, but he confessed them with shame. All his people loved him, for he was brave, unselfish, and noble-minded. He was called " the man after God's own heart," and that means that he made it his chief purpose to please God.

The people kept in their memories many of the lovely deeds which he did. One of them belonged to the time of his youth. The Philistines who had invaded the land had pressed on as far as to Bethlehem, where they built a fort and set a garrison. David and his soldiers were driven to the hills, hemmed in by the Philistines, and compelled to live in caves. There came a day of baking heat. The water springs among the hills were running dry. David remembered a clear, cool, never-ceasing well of water beside the gate of Bethlehem. He had often quenched his thirst at it when he was a boy.

As he thought of the water, he longed for it and said, " Oh, that one would give me to drink of the water of the well of Bethlehem, which is by the gate ! "

Three of his soldiers heard him, and they set off to Bethlehem. They broke through the host of the Philistines, filled a vessel with water, and brought it to him. He looked at the water for a moment, and then he poured it out upon the ground. He knew at what risk it had been brought, and he saw how deep was the love these brave men bore to him. He would not drink of it, and he said, " Be it far from me, O Lord, that I should do this ; is not this the blood of the men that went in jeopardy of their lives ? " Who would not love so noble a spirit ?

Some time afterwards, when he had become the king, he began to think about Jonathan, his friend. He called a servant of the house of Saul, and said to him, " Is there yet any of the house of Saul, that I may show him kindness, for Jonathan's sake ? " Jonathan had left behind him a little son, who was

only five years old when his father was killed. His
name was Mephibosheth. The news of the defeat
and death of Saul and Jonathan was carried to
Jonathan's house. It was feared that the Philistines
would come and ravage it. So the little boy's nurse
took him, and made haste to escape. But as she
fled, she fell, and in her fall both the little boy's
ankles were broken. They healed, but he was lame
all his life. He could not do a man's work among
the flock or in the vineyard. He could not be a
soldier.

David was told of him and sent for him. He was
now grown to be a man, and he limped into David's
presence in great fear. Mephibosheth was afraid that
David was recalling all that his grandfather, Saul, had
done when he cast a javelin at him to kill him, and
when he had hunted him on the mountains. He did
not know how tender and how kindly were David's
thoughts. As Mephibosheth fell on his face before
David, he heard, to his surprise, the king saying to
him, " Fear not : for I will surely show thee kindness for Jonathan, thy father's sake, and will restore
thee all the land of Saul, thy father, and thou shalt
eat bread at my table continually."

So Mephibosheth was given a house in Jerusalem,
and he came to the king's table like one of his sons,
and David made abundant provision for him.

As David grew older he increased in wealth and in
power, but his heart was proud and began to exult
because of his wide dominions. So he was tempted

to number the people, that he might see how great and powerful the kingdom had become.

David's heart smote him after he had numbered the people. He began to see that he would grieve God because he was depending on his armies, as the kings of the heathen did round about him. And he said to God, " I have sinned greatly in that I have done ; and now I beseech Thee, O Lord, take away the iniquity of Thy servant, for I have done very foolishly." Next morning, very early, God's prophet came to David to tell him that God was angry with him, and would punish him.

So God sent a pestilence. But after a time God was sorry for the people, and He said, " It is enough." Then came God's prophet and told him, " Go up, rear an altar unto the Lord in the threshing-floor of Araunah, the Jebuzite." That was a high spot where the wind blew, and the altar could be seen from far.

Araunah saw the king and his servants coming, and he wondered why they were climbing the hill to his threshing-floor. David said, " To buy the threshing-floor of thee, to build an altar unto the Lord, that the plague may be stayed from the people." Araunah said that David might take, without price, all that seemed good to him, and that he might have the oxen for the burnt sacrifice, and even the threshing instruments for wood to burn on the altar. But David said, " Nay ; but I will surely buy it of thee at a price : neither will I offer burnt offerings unto the Lord, my God, of that which doth cost me nothing."

That was another golden deed, and as we see his unselfish spirit, we know why he was called " the man after God's own heart."

THE WISDOM AND SPLENDOUR OF SOLOMON

After a long reign King David came to die. He called Solomon, his son, and said, " I go the way of all the earth : be thou strong, therefore, and show thyself a man : and keep the charge of the Lord thy God to walk in His ways." When he died Solomon became king. He began to rule over a wide dominion which had increased in wealth and power, and over a people at peace from all their enemies, and at full liberty to live a joyous life. David had named his son Solomon, which means the Prince of Peace, for he was glad to think that Solomon would not be a man of war, as he had been.

Solomon was young, and he trembled at the charge which had been given to him, and he feared as he thought on the task of ruling over so great a kingdom. He called the chief men among the people, and held a solemn service in a holy place at Gibeon, and offered to God a costly sacrifice of a thousand bullocks, and besought the help of God.

That night, as he slept, he dreamed, and God said to him in his dream, "Ask what I shall give thee." Solomon said, " I am but a little child ; I know not how to go out or come in. And Thy servant is in the midst of Thy people which Thou hast chosen, a

great people. Give, therefore, Thy servant an understanding heart to judge Thy people that I may discern
between good and bad." It pleased the Lord that
Solomon had asked an understanding heart, and He
said, " Behold I have done according to thy word."
Solomon awoke, and at once he went to Jerusalem,
and offered up a sacrifice, and rejoiced in the goodness of God.

A short time afterwards Solomon gave proof that
God had given him wisdom. Two women came to
his judgment seat, as the people do in the East, to
ask justice from him. Their story was that they lived
together in one house, and no one else lived in the
house with them. Each of the women had a little
baby boy. One of the mothers had overlain her child
in her sleep, and she awoke to find that it was dead.
She rose up in the darkness, and put her dead baby
into the other woman's bosom, and took away the
living child. When the other mother awoke in the
morning, she found a dead baby in her arms. But
she saw at once that the dead baby was not her own
little son. So they quarrelled, and when they came
to the king, the one woman said in reply to the other's
story, " Nay ; but the living is my son, and the dead
is thy son." The other replied, " No ; but the dead
is thy son, and the living is my son."

Solomon looked at them both for a moment, and
then he commanded, " Bring me a sword." To the
soldier who brought the sword, Solomon said, " Divide
the living child in two, and give half to the one and

half to the other." When the soldier laid hold upon the child, its real mother cried out in her anguish, " O, my Lord, give her the living child, and in no wise slay it." But the other woman, who had stolen it, said calmly, " Let it be neither mine nor thine, but divide it." The king knew at once which woman had spoken the truth, and he said, " Give her the living child, and in nowise slay it : she is the mother." When the people heard of the judgment, they saw that God had given wisdom to Solomon.

For many years Solomon reigned and his kingdom increased in splendour. He built a most beautiful temple in Jerusalem, with cedars from Lebanon in the north, and gold from Ophir in the south, and it was dedicated to God with solemn services. He raised a magnificent palace as his home, and he strengthened Jerusalem with high walls that ran round the city. He had horses and chariots and vessels on the sea which brought him gold and spices and precious stones, along with their merchandise. The fame of his wisdom and his splendour was carried into all the countries round about.

There was a notable queen, the Queen of Sheba, in the south of Arabia, who had heard the report of the wisdom of Solomon, and had been told of his riches and power and magnificence. She was a woman who loved wisdom, and she had many thoughts which troubled her. So she made a long and difficult journey to King Solomon to put questions to him about the things she could not well understand, and

to see all the wonderful buildings and the richness of
his city. She came with a great host of servants,
and with camels laden with spices and gold and
precious stones as a present to Solomon.

The king received her into his palace, and day after
day was spent in seeing the sights of Jerusalem, and
in taking counsel of Solomon's wisdom. She saw
the stately temple with its great steps of approach
and his own costly house. She took part in splendid
banquets, with dishes of gold on the table, and
an amazing abundance of provision for every one.
She saw abounding prosperity and generous feasting
served by Solomon's waiting men in rich apparel, and
she marked how happy and contented the people
were. And she found that the fame of Solomon's
wisdom was deserved, for the king answered all her
questions.

She had come thinking that she might ask questions
he could not answer, and that the report of his splendour would not be true. Now she broke out in loud
praise, and said, " It was a true report that I heard
in mine own land of thy sayings and of thy wisdom.
Behold the half was not told me : thy wisdom and
prosperity exceedeth the fame which I had heard.
Happy are thy men, happy are these thy servants,
which stand continually before thee, and that hear
thy wisdom. Blessed be the Lord thy God which
delighted in thee, to set thee on the throne of Israel."
Then she gave him a rich present, and returned to her
own land, praising the God of Israel.

THE FAITHFUL WITNESSES

Elijah on Mount Carmel

MANY years after Solomon's glorious reign there was a king of Israel named Ahab. He forsook God and began to worship Baal, who was the god of the Zidonians, a heathen tribe. He had married a heathen princess named Jezebel, and she induced him to put to death the prophets of God, and to build a temple to Baal, and to lead the people to worship him.

But there was a prophet named Elijah who lived in Gilead, across the Jordan. He was a man who loved simple things, and wore only a leathern girdle around his loins, and he was a stern and fearless believer in God. He came to Ahab to pronounce God's sentence of punishment. He stood before him and said, "As the Lord God of Israel liveth, there shall not be dew nor rain these years, but according to my word." He left the king's presence, and went down to live a lonely life beside a brook across the Jordan, and God sent ravens who brought him his food every morning and evening.

Elijah's terrible prophecy was fulfilled. Neither rain nor dew fell. The grass withered. The cattle began to die. The deepest wells dried up, and the people were starving. The brook by which Elijah lived also failed, and God told him to leave it and to take his journey westward toward the sea.

After some days he came to the gate of a city of Zidon as a poor woman was coming out of it. He asked her for a little water to quench his thirst, and a

God sent ravens who brought him food

morsel of bread to satisfy his hunger. The woman was a widow with one little son. She said that she had no bread, but only a handful of meal in a barrel, and a little oil in a cruse. Elijah told her to give him a share of the meal, when it was cooked, and he made her a comforting promise, "The barrel of meal shall not waste, neither shall the cruse of oil fail until the day that the Lord sendeth rain upon the earth." The woman found to her surprise, that every morning there was meal in the barrel, and oil in the cruse.

But the famine became unbearable. Ahab and his chief minister went out to see if they could find any springs or streams, or light upon any pastures to keep the cattle alive. It was the third year of the famine, and the whole land was burned up. Elijah left the widow's house and went to meet Ahab, and he sent him a message that he was coming. When Ahab saw Elijah and remembered that this awful drought had come upon Israel at Elijah's word, he spoke in anger, "Art thou he that troubleth Israel?" Elijah answered, " I have not troubled Israel ; but thou, and thy father's house, in that ye have forsaken the commandments of the Lord."

Elijah then offered Ahab a challenge. He asked him to call the people of Israel to the high ridge of Mount Carmel, and to gather there the eight hundred and fifty prophets of Baal.

Elijah then proposed a trial between the God of Israel and Baal. He told them to build an altar, and to take two bullocks and cut them in pieces. The priests would lay one bullock on the altar on top of the wood, but put no fire under. He would lay the other bullock on the wood, and put no fire under. Then Elijah said, " Call ye on the name of your gods, and I will call on the name of the Lord ; and the god that answereth by fire, let him be God." The people said, " It is well spoken."

So the prophets of Baal took the bullock, and dressed it, and laid it on the altar, and they called on the name of Baal, " O Baal, hear us." But there was no answer, for no voice broke the silence. They cried all forenoon, and Elijah broke in with mockery, " Cry aloud ; for he is a god : either he is talking, or he is hunting, or he is on a journey, or he sleepeth, and must be awaked." Then they cried more loudly, and cut themselves with knives, until their blood gushed out. They kept on crying until the evening, but no answer came.

Then Elijah asked the people to come nearer. He repaired the altar that had been broken down, and then made a trench round about it. He dressed the bullock, and laid it on the wood on his altar. As the sun was setting, Elijah prayed, " Lord God of Abraham, Isaac, and of Israel, let it be known this day that Thou art God in Israel, and that I am Thy servant, and that I have done all these things at Thy word. Hear me, O Lord, hear me, that this people may know that Thou art the Lord God, and that Thou hast turned their heart back again."

Then fire fell from heaven, and kindled the wood, and burned the flesh of the bullock. It blazed until it made the stones so hot that they cracked, and the fire licked up the water in the trench. The people fell on their faces and cried, " The Lord, He is the God ; the Lord, He is the God."

Ahab was standing by, and Elijah said to him. " Get thee up, eat and drink ; for there is a sound of abundance of rain." He went up with his servant to the top of the mount and they looked towards the sea. At first the sky was clear. Then a little cloud appeared. In a short time the heavens were black, and soon there was a great rain. All the people gave thanks at the coming of the rain from God, at the word of His prophet, Elijah.

ELISHA AND NAAMAN THE LEPER

Elijah the prophet was passing a field one day when he saw one of his young disciples ploughing with a yoke of oxen. His name was Elisha, and he had been taught by Elijah to believe in the God of Israel. So Elijah called him to leave his ploughing, and to come with him and he would teach him about the ways of God. Elisha left his home, and became Elijah's companion. When Elijah was taken up to heaven he gave his young disciple his own spirit, and bestowed upon him a great blessing, and so Elisha became the prophet of God to the people.

Elisha did many wonderful things. He was a man of great kindness and gentleness, and most gracious speech. He loved little children, and once when a little boy had been smitten by sunstroke in the harvest field, he brought him back to life again. At another time, when some poisonous herbs had been put into the workmen's pottage, he cast in some meal, and they could eat the pottage without harm.

H

Saul sent for David to play upon the harp.

(*See page* 98)

" *The adversary and enemy is this wicked Haman.*"

(See page 126)

" Would God my lord were with the prophet that is in Samaria ! "

(*See page* 113)

A good report of his wisdom and of his grace went through the land, and all the people loved him.

The Syrians who lived in the north were a wild and dangerous tribe. They often sent their soldiers to make raids upon the land of Israel. They had a skilful captain called Naaman, and in one of his raids on the land of Israel his soldiers had carried away a little girl, and she was given, as a slave, to Naaman's wife. But Naaman, although a captain of the Syrian host, was a leper. Leprosy is a loathsome disease, which scabs and wastes the flesh, and is incurable.

Naaman's wife had been kind to the little maid, and when she saw her master's affliction and the sorrow of her mistress, she was grieved for them. She knew that the God of Israel alone could heal the leper. She remembered Elisha, and all the merciful deeds that he had done, and she said to her mistress, " Would God my lord were with the prophet that is in Samaria ! for he would recover him of his leprosy."

Her mistress told her husband what the maid had said, and the saying was repeated to the king. The king had been deeply grieved that so fine a soldier should be so afflicted, and he said to him, " I will send a letter unto the king of Israel." The king thought that this power to heal could be only the power of the king. So he wrote a letter, and gave it to Naaman, and sent him away with many servants, and a rich present of silver, and of gold, and of changes of raiment.

Now the king had written in the letter, " Now

when this letter is come unto thee, behold I have therewith sent Naaman, my servant, unto thee that thou mayest recover him of his leprosy." When the king of Israel read the letter he rose up in alarm, and rent his clothes, and cried out, "Am I God, to kill and to make alive, that this man doth send unto me, to recover a man of his leprosy ? "

The news of the king's terror was carried to Elisha, and he sent a message to send the Syrian captain to him. So Naaman drove along the road in his grand chariot, accompanied by his servants, and stood at the door of the house of Elisha. Elisha did not come out of his house to speak to him. He merely sent a message, " Go and wash in Jordan seven times, and thy flesh shall come again to thee, and thou shalt be clean."

Naaman was angry. He said that he thought the prophet would come out of his house, and then, lifting his hand to heaven, would call on the name of his God, and touch the leprous spot, and so he would be healed. Besides, he was annoyed that the prophet had told him to wash in the Jordan, and not in the Abana and Pharpar, the two broad rivers of Damascus. He turned and went away in a rage.

But his servants were wiser than he, and they reasoned with him, " My father, if the prophet had bid thee do some great thing, wouldst thou not have done it ? How much rather then when he saith to thee, ' Wash, and be clean.' " Naaman saw that their counsel was wise. He went down to the Jordan, dipped himself seven times in its water, and came out to find that his leprosy was healed. The foul scabs had gone, and his flesh was clean and pure as the flesh of a little child.

He drove back at once to the house of Elisha. He passed in through its lowly door, and stood before the prophet, and he said, " Behold, now I know that there is no God in all the earth but in Israel : now, therefore, I pray thee, take a blessing of thy servant." As Naaman pressed the gift upon him he said, "As the Lord liveth before whom I stand, I will receive none."

Naaman began to feel that the land of Israel was holy. He asked that he might be given as much of its soil as two mules could carry. He had become a believer in God, and he wanted to worship Him, and he thought he could do that in a better way if he knelt, when he prayed, upon the earth which had been taken from the land of Israel. We can be sure that both Naaman and his wife were kind to the little maid, and that her faith in God was stronger than ever and that she served Him all her days.

DANIEL IN THE LION'S DEN

The story of the later years of the people of Israel is strange and sad. They had wicked kings and false prophets. Worst of all, they broke His commandments, and did evil, and vexed His great heart. So God allowed Nebuchadnezzar, the king of Babylon, with his great armies, to take Jerusalem, burn up its temple, and carry its people captive to Babylon.

Among the youths who were carried away to

Babylon there were four whose names we know.
They were Daniel, Hananiah, Mishael, and Azariah.
Daniel was a noble-looking youth, and every one who
knew him, felt drawn to him. He was a wonderful
scholar, and soon became known for his learning and
his skill. The king of Babylon had heard of these
four Hebrew young men, and he wished to show kindness to them. He sent a portion of the rich food
from his table, and of the wine which he drank.
Daniel would neither eat the food nor drink the wine.
The king's steward was afraid that the king would
be angry, and punish him if he saw that Daniel was
not so fair in face and strong in body, because he had
not eaten the king's dainties. But when the steward
saw that Daniel grew even finer looking, he allowed
him to eat his own simple food.

His knowledge and wisdom had become known.
He had one special gift, as Joseph had, of understanding and interpreting dreams. At one time the
king was troubled because of a strange dream which
had disturbed his sleep. What it was he could not
recall in the morning. Daniel came, and told him
both what he had dreamed, and the meaning of it.
At another time the king's son Belshazzar had seen
at a great banquet a hand write upon the wall in great
letters the words, "Mene, Mene, Tekel, Upharsin."
As he read these words his face turned white and he
trembled. Daniel was called, and he told him the
meaning of the words. So all Babylon heard of the
wondrous skill of Daniel.

This high fame of Daniel brought him into a position of power and influence. He became the first of the three governors of the land. But many of the Babylonian princes were jealous of him. They began to watch him, so as to find out some fault against him, and accuse him of some wrong-doing. They began to see that they could make a charge against him only in regard to his worship of the God of Israel. And this is how they were able to accuse him.

They went to the king at that time, whose name was Darius, to ask him to make a decree, " Whosoever shall ask a petition of any god or man for thirty days, save of thee, O king, he shall be cast into the den of lions."

Daniel knew why these evil men had framed this decree. When it was signed he saw that his time of trial was come. But he resolved that he would not cease to pray three times a day, to the God of Israel. It had been his custom to pray in his chamber before his open windows, because he looked through the open windows towards Jerusalem, the holy city of Israel. So, as usual, Daniel kneeled down, three times a day, with his windows open to Jerusalem, and gave thanks to God.

The men who had laid the plot looked up and saw Daniel praying. They went at once to King Darius, and they reminded him that he had signed the decree, and the king said, " The thing is true." Then they said, " Daniel, which is of the children of the captivity of Judah, regardeth not thee, O king, nor the decree that thou hast signed, but prays three times a day."

The king was sore displeased with himself. He saw that he had been led into this difficulty by their deceit and guile. He tried to think of some way of delivering Daniel. But although he laboured till the going down of the sun, he could not see any way of saving Daniel from the den of lions.

He gave the command, and Daniel was taken to be cast into the den of lions. The king said to him as he was being taken away, " Thy God, whom thou servest continually, He will deliver thee." Daniel was cast into the den among the lions, and a stone was rolled up to the mouth of the den, and it was sealed, both by the king and by the princes, so that no one might try to rescue Daniel during the night.

That night the king fasted in his sorrow, and he could not sleep. He rose early in the morning, and hastened to the den. He cried in with a voice of lamentation, " O Daniel, servant of the living God, is thy God, whom thou servest continually, able to deliver thee from the lions ? " Daniel's voice rang out clear and strong, " O king, live for ever. My God hath sent his angel, and shut the lions' mouths, and they have not hurt me." The king, in his gladness, commanded Daniel to be taken out of the den, and no manner of hurt was found upon him, because he had trusted in God.

But Darius was wroth with these men who had been scheming to entrap him, and had made him sign this foolish decree. So he commanded that they should be brought and cast, with their wives and children, into the den of lions. This time the lions' mouths were not shut, for they had the mastery over them, and broke their bones in pieces. Then the king made a decree, " That in every dominion of my kingdom men tremble before the God of Daniel, for He is the living God and steadfast for ever."

THE FIERY FURNACE

When Nebuchadnezzar, the King of Babylon, conquered all the nations round about him, he spoiled them of their wealth and treasures, and carried away many captives to his great city beside the river. But he was a wise king, and he showed his wisdom in educating and training for his service any of the youths among his captives, who showed promise of ability.

In this way he chose Daniel and his three companions from among the youth of the Hebrews. Daniel rose to be one of the chief governors in Babylon, and his companions were all promoted to high office. The men of Babylon were jealous of them, and laid plots to get them put to death. In the same way as King Darius was entrapped to put Daniel in the lions' den, so they contrived a plan to cast the other three Hebrew youths into a fiery furnace, and this is how it fell out.

Nebuchadnezzar had become high-minded and proud of his power and glory. He began to think that he was a god. So he commanded his goldsmiths to make an enormous golden image, seventy feet high, and to set it upon the broad plain outside the walls of Babylon. He gathered round the image all his princes and counsellors and the chief men of his provinces. Then he sent out a proclamation to all the nations and the peoples he had conquered, that when a great music on many instruments was played, they should fall down and worship the golden image. He added an awful punishment for those who would not obey. " Whoso falleth not down and worshippeth shall, the same hour, be cast into the midst of a burning fiery furnace."

These three Hebrew young men were among the great multitude on the plain. The king had shown them much favour, and he had changed their Hebrew names to Shadrach, Meshach, and Abednego. But they did not bow down before the golden image. The men who were watching them told the king, and he was full of rage and fury. He called them to his presence, and said that he would give them a second chance, and that all would be well if they would go out to the plain and fall down before the golden image. Then he said, " But if ye worship not, ye shall be cast, the same hour, into the midst of a burning fiery furnace ; and who is that God that shall deliver you out of my hands ? "

He said this because he guessed that they were

trusting in the God of Israel. So they were, for they answered, "If it be so, our God whom we serve is able to deliver us from the burning fiery furnace, and He will deliver us out of thine hand, O king. But if not, be it known unto thee, O king, that we will not serve thy gods, nor worship the golden image

The Site of Babylon.

which thou hast set up." At this reply Nebuchadnezzar became so moved with anger that he scowled upon them. He gave orders to heat the fiery furnace seven times more than usual, and to bind the young men in their garments, and to throw them into the very midst of the flames of the furnace. So they were seized and bound and carried to the furnace and cast into it. The blazing flames burned so fiercely that the soldiers who took the three young men to the furnace were burned to death.

I

As the king sat to look on at this dreadful scene, he saw the three youths walking in the furnace, unbound and unharmed. And he saw a fourth young man walking with them who seemed to be as holy as the Son of God. He rose up from his seat in astonishment and he spoke to his counsellors, " Did not we cast three men bound into the midst of the fire ? " They answered and said to him, " True, O king." He answered and said, " Lo, I see four men, loose, walking in the midst of the fire, and they have no hurt, and the form of the fourth is like the Son of God."

Then the king came down from his seat, and drew near to the great door of the burning fiery furnace, and called to the three young men, " Shadrach, Meshach, and Abednego, ye servants of the Most High God, come forth, and come hither." They came up out of the fiery furnace, and when they came to Nebuchadnezzar it was seen that not a hair of their heads was singed, neither were their coats changed, and not even the smell of fire came from them.

Nebuchadnezzar was completely changed in mind. He no longer desired men to think him a god, or to worship a golden image. He made a decree that any people or nation which would speak evil of the God of Israel, would be destroyed, and their houses made into a dunghill, for, said he, " There is no other God that can deliver after this sort." Then he turned to the three brave young men, and raised them to higher offices in his province of Babylon.

The Heroic Faith of Queen Esther

When Jerusalem was destroyed until it became a heap of stones, the Hebrew people were carried away as captives into many lands. Some were taken to Babylon, and others were taken across the broad plain into Persia. But they did not forget their God. They knew how they had sinned against Him, and many of them prayed earnestly to Him, for they could not, and they would not, forget Jerusalem.

Among those who were deported to Persia, there was a Jewish family, the chief member of which at this time was a devout man named Mordecai. He had a niece, whose father and mother were dead, and he took her into his home to live in his household. She was a beautiful young girl, modest in all her conduct, and was a true believer in God.

Now the King of the Persians was angry with his wife and he sent her away. Then when Esther was brought to him he was so charmed with her beauty, and her natural and simple manner, that he made her the queen. Her uncle Mordecai was somewhat anxious in his mind about her fate in the king's palace, and he was afraid that if he came to know she was a Jewess, he might not treat her kindly. So he told her not to disclose her birth. But he walked in the outer court every day, very eager to hear news of Esther.

In the king's court there was a man named Haman, belonging to the fierce heathen tribe of the Amalekites,

who were always enemies of Israel. He hated the
Jews, because they were God's people, and he looked
at Mordecai with eyes of anger, because Mordecai
would not bow down to him. He conceived a wicked
plot to induce the king to make a decree, that all the
Jews in his wide dominion should be put to death.
He offered the great sum of ten thousand talents of
silver to pay the cost of this awful butchery. He gave
as his reason to the king, that " their laws are divers
from all people ; neither keep they the king's laws,
therefore it is not for the king's profit to suffer them."
But his real reason was that he hated the Jews, and
he thought that, if this decree to slay them were
issued, Mordecai would be slain along with his people.

When Mordecai heard the decree he rent his clothes,
put on sackcloth, cast ashes on his head, and went
out into the chief streets of the city, and cried with a
loud and bitter cry. He came at last to the king's
gate pouring forth his lamentations. Esther's maids
told her of his weeping. She sent new clothing to
him, but he would not wear it. Then she sent to ask
why he was in such grief. He gave her messenger a
copy of the decree, and asked her to go to the king
and to beg him not to enforce its cruel design.

Esther's heart quailed. She was not sure of the
king's favour, and she knew that if she went into his
presence without being called, she might be put to
death, and she sent back a message that she could not
speak to the king.

Mordecai told the messenger to answer Esther,

" Think not with thyself that thou shalt escape in the king's house, more than all the Jews." He knew that when once the massacre had begun, no Jew or Jewess would be spared anywhere, and he added the question, " Who knoweth, whether thou art come to the kingdom for such a time as this ? " He meant to say that the very reason why God had exalted her to be queen was that she might protect and save His people. Esther stood very still for a moment. Then she sent back an answer that all the Jews should fast for her three days, and three nights, and she would go into the king. She knew she was facing death, but she said, " If I perish, I perish."

Esther put on her most beautiful garments and went into the king's presence. He lifted his eyes and looked upon her with pleasure, and she knew that she had found favour. He asked why she had come, and she told him that she wished to invite the king and Haman to come to a banquet with her. As they sat together that day the king said, " What is thy petition, Queen Esther ? and it shall be granted thee : and what is thy request ? even to the half of the kingdom it shall be performed." Esther answered that she wished both the king and Haman to come to a banquet on the morrow, and there she would tell him what was her petition and her request.

When Haman heard himself invited to this banquet, he thought that his hour of triumph had come. As he went home, to tell his wife of the honour to be paid to him, he saw Mordecai, and his eyes flashed anger upon him. In his house he told the story of the coming honour, but he said that the very sight of Mordecai tormented him. His wife said to him that he should prepare a gallows, and, at the banquet on the morrow, speak to the king that he should hang Mordecai on it.

That night the king could not sleep. He summoned a reader who read to him out of the book of the history of his kingdom. The reader came to a passage where it was written that Mordecai had discovered a plot against the king's life. He asked if Mordecai had been rewarded, and when he found that nothing had been given to him, he told Haman to clothe him in royal apparel, set him on the king's horse, put the king's crown upon his head, and send him to be shown to the people through the city. The proclamation to be made was, " Thus shall it be done unto the man whom the king delighteth to honour."

Haman went home with a heart bitter with the gall of his hate. But worse was to follow. When he went into the banquet and the king asked Esther what was her petition, she answered, " If I have found favour in thy sight, O king, let my life be given me at my petition, and my people at my request; for we are sold, I and my people, to be destroyed, to be slain, and to perish." The king said, " Who is he, and where is he, that durst presume in his heart to do so ? " Esther pointed to Haman and said, " The adversary and enemy is this wicked Haman." The

king's wrath broke out, and he gave orders to hang
Haman on the gallows he had prepared for Mordecai,
for his chamberlain had told him of Haman's wicked
purpose in preparing the gallows. So God's people
were saved from the cruel massacre, through the noble
courage and the heroic faith of Queen Esther.

The story of Queen Esther is one of the loveliest

The Tomb of Mordecai and Esther in Persia.

of the many golden deeds of the Bible. It will never
be forgotten. Her name is beautiful, both in its
sound and its meaning. It was the name of the
loveliest star in the heavens—the star Venus. Her
life was fair, and full of loyalty to her uncle Mordecai,
and to her husband, and to her people, because her
heart was loyal to God. Many beautiful deeds are
recorded as done by the women of the Bible. We

remember young Miriam watching among the rushes on the bank of the Nile to see what would happen to her baby brother, placed in the ark of bulrushes. We love the story of Ruth, who left her home and her people to go with Naomi to endure the poverty and the loneliness of a strange land, and to live among a people who would not look upon her with kindly eyes. We are made glad by the story of the little Hebrew maid, who was carried away to Damascus and became the servant of the wife of Naaman, the Syrian soldier. But Esther and her great service outshine them all. She made a noble sacrifice. She risked all she had. She braved death, for she knew that was the most likely thing to happen to her. Then, she was young, with all her life before her. She was a queen in a place of power. She had a lovely home and everything that could make her days full of delight. It was a great trial to her to be asked to take the part of her people. We know how it troubled her mind, and how it perplexed her spirit, when the course she took was pressed upon her. She saw how it might end, and in her youth, with no one to be her companion, the trial was severe. Yet when she had prayed, and cast her care upon God, she went forward, risking all. In her troubled words we have the echoes of her fear. God gave her light to see her way, and she stepped out upon it, to save her people at all cost to herself. There is no one more like Jesus, in His sacrifice, than Esther, the Queen.

THE CHILDHOOD AND YOUTH
OF JESUS

MARY, THE MOTHER OF JESUS

THE greatest event of all time is the coming into the world of Jesus, the eternal Son of God. The story of His birth is the most wonderful and the most beautiful story in the world. He came to be born of a woman, and to be a little child, that He might be the King over all men, and win them back to God by His love and grace. And He was sent to the Hebrew people, because God chose them for Himself. They once were known by the name of the Israelites, but when Jesus came they were known as the Jews, because their great city was Jerusalem, in the land of Judah.

Now there lived in the little town of Nazareth, in the north of Palestine, a family with a daughter named Mary. This family belonged to the royal race of David, and had come to Nazareth from Bethlehem. There they had lived for many years as plain working folk. Mary was a simple, humble girl, and Joseph, to whom she was about to be married, was the village carpenter.

One day, when she was sitting alone, the angel Gabriel was sent from God with a strange message.

As the angel came into the house, she lifted her eyes in wonder. And then she heard him say, "Hail, thou art highly favoured, the Lord is with thee; blessed art thou among women." The sight of the angel made her tremble, but his strange words troubled her mind, for she did not know what this salutation meant. When the angel saw her anxious face he spoke again, calling her by her name, and giving her a fuller message. "Fear not, Mary; for thou hast found favour with God. Behold thou shalt bring forth a Son, and shall call His name Jesus. He shall be great and shall be called the Son of the Highest: and the Lord God shall give unto Him the throne of His father David: and of His kingdom there shall be no end."

No one in Nazareth knew of this visit of the angel, and Mary kept his message as a secret to herself. But she had a cousin, named Elisabeth, who lived among the hills of Judah, five days' journey away. So she set out to visit her, and after a long travel she entered Elisabeth's home to tell her the burden of her heart. But before Mary could speak, Elisabeth welcomed her with the words, "Blessed art thou among women: and whence is this to me, that the mother of my Lord should come to me?" Then Mary, who had been remembering Hannah, when she was told that she would have a little son and call him Samuel, broke out into a song, "My soul doth magnify the Lord, and my spirit doth rejoice in God my Saviour. Behold, from henceforth all generations

shall call me blessed." After three months she
went back to Nazareth, taking up her simple duties,
but never forgetting God's wonderful messages, for
we are told, " She kept all these sayings in her
heart."

At this time the Roman Emperor made a decree
that all the citizens of the empire should be enrolled

There were shepherds keeping watch over their flocks.

and numbered. For this purpose every one was
commanded to go to the city to which he belonged.
So Joseph and Mary set out to go to Bethlehem.
Every road in Palestine was thronged with travellers,
and every inn was crowded with guests. When they
came to Bethlehem they found that there was no
room for them in the inn. They went up and

down its stony streets, looking for a lodging for Mary in her hour of need. But they were compelled to be content with one of the stalls in the courtyard and stable of the inn, where the horses and other animals of the travellers were sheltered and fed.

On that night, and in that rude shelter, Jesus was born. No one ever had a more humble place of birth than a cattle stall, or a meaner cradle than its manger. But Mary took her little son, and, after the custom of the time, she wrapped him round with swaddling bands, and then she laid him in her bosom. Joseph waited upon her with a tender affection, and, shortly after the midnight hour, a silence fell upon the little company in the stall. No one would have believed that this was the most wonderful event of all time's history.

On Christmas Eve

There was silence in the little town of Bethlehem on that night when Jesus was born. The people slept their sound sleep, not dreaming that the little child, who was the Son of God, had been born in one of the stalls of the inn. But there were shepherds keeping watch over their flocks in the high pasture fields the whole night long.

So to these shepherds, speaking together of God and His love, and not to the learned scribes in Jerusalem, God sent an angel. Suddenly the darkness of the night was broken in upon by a great light which shone round about them. They were in terror at this sudden brightness. Then there came the voice of the angel, " Fear not ; for, behold, I bring you good tidings of great joy, which shall be to all people, for unto you is born this day, in the city of David, a Saviour which is Christ the Lord."

This amazing message was so strange that these simple shepherd men did not know what to think, and could not understand this declaration about the child that had been born to-day. So the angel gave them a sign by which they would find the little child. "And this shall be a sign unto you ; ye shall find the babe wrapped in swaddling clothes, lying in a manger." Then suddenly a host of shining angels came out from heaven, and joined the angel who had spoken, and they sang a great song, " Glory to God in the highest, and on earth peace, goodwill toward men." Then the angels went away, and the shepherds were left alone in the still, dark night.

These good men were at a loss what to think about these angels, and their songs, and about what to do. So, after some conversation with each other, they thought they would put the sign given by the angel to a test. So they said, " Let us now go, even unto Bethlehem, and see this thing which is come to pass, which the Lord hath made known unto us."

They left their sheep and hastened down the hill-side where they had seen the angel, and came to the gate of Bethlehem. They found everything silent, for the gate was always shut at night. They aroused the watchman, and they told him why they had come, and they passed swiftly up the steep street to the inn, for they knew that they might find the little child in one of its mangers. They saw the light in the stall where Mary was lying with her babe on her bosom. They went in, and looked with amazement, for there they saw the babe wrapped in swaddling clothes, and lying in its manger cradle.

As they came back down the street, the morning light was breaking in the sky. The people of Bethlehem were rising from their rest and slumber, and the streets were full of men and women going about their tasks and passing forth to their labour. They told them the story of the heavenly angels, their strange words, and the sign they had given. As the people heard that the angels had said that this child was to be a saviour, and was that Christ of whom all the prophets had spoken, we are told that " they wondered."

We know why they wondered. For when they thought of a king, they thought of one who should come to some great family, and should live in grandeur, and should put on costly robes and rule with power.

" They were all looking for a king,
    To slay their foes, and lift them high.
Thou camest, a little baby thing
    That made a woman cry."

Every Christmas Eve we are all called around His cradle, and we are all reminded of the lowliness of Jesus, and of His laying aside His heavenly greatness, that He might be " a Saviour which is Christ the Lord." Only Mary, the mother of Jesus, of all those who saw Him, knew the great promise which had been made to her about Jesus. But she told no one, although she brooded over them every day and every night. " Mary kept all these things and pondered them in her heart."

THE PRESENTATION IN THE TEMPLE

The name of a little child is often chosen before the day of its birth. As we know, an angel had said to Mary that her little son should be named Jesus, because He was to be the Saviour. So eight days after He was born, that name was given to Him, and all the world knows it and loves it now.

But there was another law among the Jews which Mary was eager to keep. That law required that the first-born son should be offered to the service of God. When the child was offered the parents brought a sacrifice with them. If they were rich, they gave a lamb. If they were poor, they gave two turtle-doves, or two young pigeons. So forty days after Jesus was born, when He had become a strong and beautiful child, Joseph placed Mary and her little son upon his ass, and he walked by their side, as they made the journey from Bethlehem to Jerusalem.

The chief glory of Jerusalem was neither its fine situation on a hill with deep valleys on three sides, nor its high walls and massive gates. It was its splendid temple built of great stones and costly timber, and richly adorned with gold. In the temple a daily service was held, and those who loved to worship God went up every day at the hour of prayer.

Among their number there was an old man named Simeon. He was often sad when he thought of the great days of David and Solomon, and he longed and prayed for the coming of the king who should rule again in Jerusalem.

On that day when Joseph and Mary entered Jerusalem and went up to the temple, Simeon was praying, as usual, in the Holy Place. After he had offered his prayer he looked round upon the people who were passing in at the temple gate. He saw Mary, with a little child in her arms, and Joseph accompanying her, carrying his basket with the two young pigeons. These things told him that they had come to present their child to God, and that they were poor village people. But God spoke to him in his heart, that this child was to be the King of Israel. Simeon made his way to Mary, took the little child in his arms, and lifting his eyes to heaven he prayed, amidst a perfect silence, in this way :—

" Lord, now lettest Thou Thy servant depart in peace, according to Thy word : for mine eyes have seen Thy salvation, which Thou hast prepared before the face of all people ; a light to lighten the Gentiles, and the glory of Thy people Israel."

While Simeon was speaking to Mary, there came into the temple court a very aged woman whose name was Anna. She was nearly a hundred years old, and she was one of Simeon's companions at the hour of daily prayer. She was deeply moved by what Simeon

They made the journey from Bethlehem to Jerusalem.

had said. As she looked at Mary and the child Jesus in her arms, she broke out in thanksgiving to God, and she began to speak of that Saviour King for whose coming the people of God were longing.

After Simeon and Anna had bestowed their blessing upon the little child, Joseph and Mary passed on to present Him " according to the law of the Lord."

Mary gave Jesus into Joseph's arms, and he went on from the outer court to the inner court, and knelt down before the altar. He gave the two young pigeons to the priest, and they were sacrificed as a thank offering to God, and the priest took the little child in his arms, and blessed Him in the name of God.

THE STAR IN THE EAST

Some time after Jesus was born a company of travellers from the East journeyed along the Damascus road, and passed into Jerusalem by its gate. Their leaders were three men, rich and learned and wise. They came with a large number of servants riding on camels, and they bore a costly present of gold and frankincense and myrrh, for these are the gifts which, in the East, were offered to a king, to show loyalty and to pay him honour.

These men were called Magi, which means Wise Men, who know more than others. They were skilled in the movement of the stars. On every clear dark night they went up, after midnight, to the top of high towers and looked abroad upon the heavens.

One night, as they were looking up into the heavens, they discovered a new star. Night after night they watched this star, and they marked where it rose and where it set. They said to each other that this new star was the sign and token of the coming of a new king. They marked it passing right over Jerusalem, and they declared that there had been born, in Palestine, a new King of the Jews.

So three of these Magi were sent off to visit Jerusalem. As they passed into the city they spoke at once to the people, for they supposed that every one would know where this baby king had been born. They put their question, " Where is He that is born King of the Jews ? For we have seen His star in the east, and are come to worship Him."

The arrival of the Wise Men and their strange question, along with the excited minds of the people, came to the ears of Herod the king. He was still more concerned. He was a wicked king, and he knew that the Jews hated him and his rule, and he was somewhat fearful of this talk about a little child who was to be the King of the Jews. So he gathered the priests and the learned teachers of the Jews, and he asked them where the king, whom every Jew was expecting, should be born. They answered him by repeating the words of one of the prophets, " In Bethlehem of Judea : for thus it is written by the prophet : And thou, Bethlehem, in the land of Juda, art not the least among the princes of Juda : for out of thee shall come a governor, that shall rule My people Israel."

Herod sent the priests away, and he secretly called the Wise Men to him. He asked them all about the star, and its rising and setting, and they told him what they had seen, and what they believed this new star to foretell. He sent them out to Bethlehem and said, " Go and search diligently for the young child : and when ye have found Him, bring me word again, that I may come and worship Him also." Herod did not mean to worship Jesus. He meant to kill Him, so as to prevent Him becoming the king.

That night the three Wise Men went out, as usual, to look into the heavens. As they looked they saw the star, and as they watched its motion, they saw that it moved slowly, and stood over Bethlehem. Bethlehem is six miles away from Jerusalem. So, with their camels and their attendants, they rode out to find the child. The Wise Men entered the house, and when they saw the child, they fell down and worshipped Him. Then they took their treasure chests from the camels, and laid down, at the feet of Jesus, their gold, and frankincense, and myrrh. These were the first gifts given to Jesus as a king.

On that night God warned them, in their dreams, not to return to Jerusalem and to Herod. So they mounted their camels and took their journey back to the East by another way. God also spoke to Joseph that same night, and He warned him that they should leave Bethlehem, and flee into Egypt and stay there until Herod died. So Joseph rose at once, and in the early morning he set out along that desert road that leads from Palestine to Egypt, obeying God's command, " Be thou there until I bring thee word : for Herod will seek the young child to destroy Him."

Herod waited for the return of the Wise Men, and

when he learned that they had gone back to their own land without letting him know, he was in a fury of anger. He felt that he had been mocked by them. In his wrath he resolved on an awful crime. He sent soldiers to slay all the children that were in Bethlehem and all the country round about it, who were two years old, or under two years old. In that way he thought he would kill the child Jesus among them. It was a shocking massacre, and any one who had passed through Bethlehem would have found all the mothers of Bethlehem weeping and wailing because of their little children, and unable to be comforted because of their anguish and their sorrow.

THE BOYHOOD OF JESUS

When Joseph and Mary came back from Egypt, they did not return to Bethlehem. They went north to Nazareth where they had lived before. There Joseph took up his trade of a carpenter, and Mary was busy all day long in the simple tasks of her home. So it came to pass that Jesus spent his boyhood, and nearly all his life, in the little far-away town of Nazareth.

Every boy must go to school, and Jesus entered His first school by His mother's side. He saw her bake the daily bread. He saw her spread the table for the common meal. He saw her washing, with care, both the inside and the outside of every cup and platter. He saw her light the candle to give light to all in the house. And He saw her, with her troubled face, when she was sweeping the house to find the coin that she had lost. But better still, He saw her kneel in prayer to God, and never forgot the evening hour, when she took Him beside her and taught Him His psalm.

As soon as He was old enough He went to the village school. He had no little easy lesson books, with pictures, as we have now. The school was held in the synagogue, which was the name of the church, and the only lesson book was the Bible. No child had books of his own, for the Bible was a large roll kept by the teacher. He read it out to the scholars, verse by verse, and they repeated it until they knew it by heart. What Jesus loved to learn were the stories of the Hebrew people, the sweet psalms and songs of the psalmists, and, most of all, the wondrous ways of His own Father in heaven.

As every boy and girl knows, there is a more delightful school than any taught by teachers, however wise and kind they may be. Jesus loved to walk in the fields, where He saw the vines bringing forth grapes, and the fig-trees laden with fruit. He watched the shepherds high up on the pasture fields, calling their sheep by their names, and He saw them carrying the lambs, when they were weary, in their arms. In the spring-time He marked the lilies covering the earth with a carpet of dazzling beauty, and the sparrows building their nests under the eaves. In the autumn He saw the corn being gathered like a harvest of gold.

In after days, when He spoke of God's holiness, and of God's love and care, He remembered all He had learned in this school, and retold the story in His parables and counsels.

But as He grew older He learned His trade. Every Jewish boy was expected to have some useful occupation. Joseph was the village carpenter, and his workshop, with its bench and its tools, was next door to his house. The carpenter of those days did not only build houses. He made carts, and ploughs, and yokes for the necks of the oxen who drew the ploughs and the wagons. He made tables and chairs, and all the furniture of the village homes. That was why, when He went out to teach and to preach to the people, some of the learned men said in scorn, " Is not this the carpenter ? " The proud Jews could not bear the thought that their king, or even one of their teachers, could be so lowly and so humble as Jesus was.

Now the Bible tells us almost nothing more about the years Jesus spent in Nazareth. Only this is set down. "And Jesus increased in wisdom and stature and in favour with God and man." That means that in patience and in meekness, with simple obedience and quiet industry, Jesus grew to be a true child of the Heavenly Father.

But there is one story which gives us the secret of His life. There comes a time when every boy and girl leaves childhood behind, and begins to think new thoughts and to have new desires. So when Jesus was twelve years old Joseph and Mary thought Him old enough to take part in the great Jewish feast of the Passover, and He went up with them to Jerusalem.

This Passover Feast was held once a year in the temple, at Jerusalem. It recalled that strange night, so long ago, when the people were gathered together to leave Egypt, and to go out into the wilderness. By God's command each family slew a lamb, sprinkled its blood on the doorsteps of the house, and stood waiting the command to march out of Egypt. They were told that God's angel of death would be abroad that night, and would smite the first-born of the Egyptians. But He would pass over the houses where He saw the doorposts sprinkled with blood. Once a year Joseph and Mary went up to attend the feast, and now they took Jesus with them.

How eager and how excited Jesus must have been as He entered Jerusalem. Now He saw the temple with His eyes, and took part in the Feast of which He had heard. He was so delighted and held that, when Joseph and Mary and their many friends set out to return to Nazareth, He stayed behind. He was not missed during the hours of the day, for they supposed that He was in the company of some of their companions. But at night He could not be found, and Joseph and Mary turned back, with fearful hearts, to search for Him.

After three days they found Him in the temple standing in the midst of the learned men. They had been asking Him questions, and rejoicing in His wise

O.O.S.　　　　　　　　　　　　　　　　　　　　　　　　K

*They took their treasure chests from the camels, and laid down, at the
feet of Jesus, their gold, and frankincense, and myrrh.*

(*See page* 140)

" Behold thy father and I have sought thee sorrowing."

(*See page* 145)

" Follow Me, and I will make you fishers of men."

(*See page* 152)

answers. He had asked them questions, and they were astonished at His knowledge and understanding. But Jesus had a deeper joy than they had known of. He had passed through that solemn hour, which every boy and girl should know, when they hear God's voice in their hearts and they know themselves to be children of the Father in heaven.

When Joseph and Mary found Him, His mother broke out in her surprise and sorrow, " Son, why hast Thou thus dealt with us ? behold Thy father and I have sought Thee sorrowing." Jesus looked up and said, " How is it that ye sought Me ? Wist ye not that I must be in My Father's house ? " Yet He went with them, and, for eighteen years, lived in a humble and gracious obedience in the home in Nazareth.

JESUS BEGINS HIS MINISTRY

JESUS LEAVES NAZARETH

THE quiet years, with their simple duties, which Jesus lived at Nazareth, came to an end. The time had come when He must show Himself to the people as the promised Messiah. He found that His way had been prepared by a great prophet whose name was John the Baptist. John had so stirred the hearts of all the people who had heard him that they began to wonder if he was not the promised Saviour. But John knew that he was only the herald of the King, and his work was to point out Jesus to the people, and prepare them to receive Him.

But he was early brought to see how wicked many of the people were, and how false to God were their priests and Scribes. His young spirit was vexed that the old Hebrew devotion to the will of God had passed away. So he left Jerusalem and went out into the desert to lead a stern and lonely life. He had no roof over his head except the blue sky. The only bed he lay on was the heath of the wilderness. His companions were the wild beasts. His clothing was a coat of camel's hair. His food was the locust bean sweetened with the honey of the wild bees of the wilderness. There he brooded in silence over the evil lives of the people, and prayed to God for the coming of a righteous king.

Then he began to preach to the people. He did not speak in the temple court or in the streets. He began to proclaim his message in the wilderness. But soon men began to tell each other of this prophet of the desert with his loud clear voice and his rousing appeals. Then the people began to go out to hear him, and the whole city was moved by his message, until even the priests and Scribes whom he rebuked were found listening to the stern reproaches he uttered.

It was a strange sight to see this man of the desert standing up to call men to return to the old faith. But he saw that the people had been living evil lives. He saw that too many were speaking good words and yet doing evil deeds. He saw that even the priests were not true and sincere. For that reason, his great demand was, " Repent, for the kingdom of heaven is at hand." As he spoke men and women became ashamed of their sins, and even bold men trembled. They confessed that they had been living wicked lives, and they came to John to ask him what they should do.

Among those who went out into the wilderness, and then down to the Jordan, there were many from Galilee. Jesus also was found among them. He listened to John's preaching and was glad to see the great revival. He spoke to John, and John soon learned that Jesus knew God, the Father, and loved

Him and served Him far better than any one else had done. So when Jesus said that He would be baptized along with the others, John forbade Him, saying, " I have need to be baptized of Thee, and comest Thou to me ? " But Jesus said, " Suffer it to be so now : for thus it becometh us to fulfil all righteousness."

Then a strange thing happened. As Jesus came up out of the water, the heavens opened and God's spirit, hovering over Him like a pure white dove, lighted upon Him. Then a voice from heaven spoke, " This is My beloved Son, in whom I am well pleased."

Jesus now knew that He would no longer live in Nazareth. God had called Him to go and tell the people of His love and care, and at last to die for their sins as the Lamb of God. It was a solemn call which moved Him to the depths, so He went away alone into the wilderness to fast and to pray. There He was tempted by the Evil One. At one time He was tempted to make stones into bread, and to use His divine power for Himself. At another He was tempted to fling Himself down from a high pinnacle of the temple, so as to astonish the people. At another time He was tempted to fall down and worship the Evil One, so as to gain worldly power. But He remembered God, and God's word to Him, and He did not yield. After He had spent forty days in the wilderness He came forth as God's sinless Son to do the work which God had given Him to do.

THE FIRST DISCIPLES

Among those who had gone out to hear John in the wilderness, and then down to the Jordan to be baptized of him, there were five young men who were Galileans. They were all fishermen who cast their nets and caught the fish of the Sea of Galilee. They had heard of the fame of John the Baptist and of the crowds who went out to the wilderness to hear him preach.

John saw these five young men, and he marked their earnest faces, and, when they made themselves known to him, they became his disciples. Day by day they sat with him in the quiet hours. He walked and talked with them by the way. They became his companions, and he taught them the deep things of God, and prepared them to know Jesus, and to serve Him when He came.

There was one of John's prophecies which they believed, but did not fully understand. They knew that the people must repent before they could receive their king. But they did not understand what kind of king Jesus would be, or how He would make Himself known. But when Jesus came to be baptized, and when they heard Him speak, and saw the dove descending on His head, and heard the voice that said, " This is my beloved Son," they began to wonder if He were the promised king.

John the Baptist soon made that clear. Walking one day with two of these five young men, whose names were John and Andrew, they met Jesus by the way. John stopped and looked at Jesus and said again, "Behold the Lamb of God." These two young men at once followed Jesus. They were greatly drawn to Him by His gentle bearing, His look of stainless holiness, and His eyes so full of wisdom and of kindness.

They walked some distance behind Him, but then Jesus turned, as He heard their footsteps, and He said to them, "What seek ye?" They answered, "Master, where dwellest Thou?"

Now it is John, one of these two young men, who tells us this story. He never forgot his first meeting with Christ. It was, he says, about four o'clock in the afternoon when Jesus turned and spoke to them, and when they asked Him where He dwelt, and He said, "Come and see." It was a poor lodging, perhaps only a tent, or the shelter of some tree by the river bank. But they went with Him, and they stayed all that night with Jesus. John does not report what Jesus said to them. But we know from what happened afterwards, that as they sat through the long hours, He told them that God loved the world, and that He had sent His Son to be the light of the world, and the lover and seeker of the lost. As Jesus spoke John and Andrew saw Him to be the promised Saviour, and they bowed down to worship Him. They were the first believers in Jesus Christ.

In the morning they went out to find their companions. They were thrilling with a new joy and kindling with a new hope. Andrew found his own brother, Simon, and he broke out with the cry, " We have found the Messiah," which is the Jewish name for Christ. He brought his brother Simon to Jesus, and that was the great day of Simon's life.

Jesus now crossed the Jordan to go back along the road to Galilee. As He went He found Philip, another

The Lake of Galilee

of the five young men, on his way back to his home beside the Lake of Galilee. As they walked and spoke together, Jesus asked him to follow Him, as John and Andrew and Peter had done, and he became another of Christ's disciples.

Now Philip had a friend named Nathanael. He was a shy, tender-hearted young man, who used to go to the shadow of a fig-tree that he might pray to God in secret. He had been with the others to listen to John the Baptist, but he did not know what Jesus had said to them. Philip went to see him and told him, "We have found Him of whom Moses and the law and the prophets did write, Jesus of Nazareth." Nathanael knew Nazareth, and he knew that it was not a likely place to send forth a prophet of God. So he asked, "Can there any good thing come out of Nazareth?" Philip knew that, if only he would see and hear Jesus, he would believe in Him, so he said, "Come and see." As Nathanael was taken to Jesus and had come quite near, Jesus said of him, "Behold an Israelite indeed, in whom there is no guile." Nathanael was surprised at this saying. But after they had spoken together, he also worshipped Jesus, and he said, "Thou art the Son of God; Thou art the King of Israel."

These five, John, and Andrew, and Peter, Philip, and Nathanael, were the first disciples of Jesus. For a time they went back to their own homes and launched their fishing boats again, and lived the old life. But they were all changed men. Jesus had called them to Himself and His service. There came a day, when Jesus went down to the Sea of Galilee. He found them mending their nets. He stood and said to them, "Follow Me, and I will make you fishers of men." So they left their nets and followed Him. To-day, all the world knows their names, and holds them in loving memory.

Turning Water into Wine

It was a three days' journey from the Jordan, where John was preaching and baptizing, to Nazareth, where Jesus lived.   He reached home in time to attend a wedding in Cana, to which He and His disciples had been invited.   Cana was only a few miles from Nazareth, and the bridegroom was a kinsman of Mary.

The wedding feast was held, as is the custom in the East, in the house of the bridegroom.   They were poor people, and as there were so many guests, the supply of wine ran short before the feast was over. Mary saw what was happening, and she went to Jesus and said softly, " They have no wine."   She went to Him because she knew how kind He was, and she had never asked Him for help, without help being given.

Now Jesus made a strange answer.   He said to Mary, " Woman, what have I to do with thee ?   Mine hour is not yet come."   But we must not think that Jesus spoke rudely or unkindly.   The word " woman " was used in those days as we use the word " lady," and is a respectful address.   And when Jesus said, " Mine hour is not yet come," He showed how strained and how intent He was about the great service He was soon to begin for God and His kingdom.

But His mother knew how kind He was, and she felt sure that He would do something to show His kindness.   So she said, " Whatsoever He saith unto you, do it." She had proved how willing He was to do good to every one, and now and again she found her trust in Him was justified. For, as Jesus knew the shame that would fall upon the givers of the feast, the taunts they might have to bear, and the unkind gossip of the country side, He used His divine power in an act of loving service and thoughtful kindliness.

There were set, along the wall of the room, six large stone water pots. Before the feast began they had been filled with water for the washing of the feet of the guests after their journey, and the washing of their hands before sitting down to the feast. Now they were empty. Jesus commanded the attendants, " Fill the water pots with water." The attendants wondered at this strange command, but they remembered what Mary had said, and they filled them up to the brim. Then said Jesus, " Draw out now, and bear unto the governor of the feast."

When the governor of the feast, who was in charge of the ceremonies, tasted the wine, although he did not know that Jesus had made it, he was delighted. He called the bridegroom, and, in a pleasant jest, he said that at most feasts they gave the best wine first, and he added, " Thou hast kept the good wine until now." His disciples, who knew that He had made the wine, saw how wonderful was His goodness, and they believed more surely than before.

Jesus did not go back to Nazareth, but went down to Capernaum along with His disciples, and He took His mother with Him. Then, as the time of the

Passover Feast was at hand, He went up to Jerusalem to attend it.

He had seen, too often, how many observed the Passover without reverence, or without a true joy in God. Now, when He knew Himself to be God's Messiah, and God's messenger, and when He remembered that the temple was God's House, He resolved to make an endeavour to keep it holy.

He passed in to the outer court and He stood still to look at the traffic which was being carried on, and to listen to the clamour of the bargaining. The temple services required sheep, and lambs, and oxen, and doves for the sacrifices. The strangers who came from all parts of the world required to exchange their foreign money, to pay the temple tax to the priests. In former times they had carried on their buying and selling outside the temple gate. Now they had driven in their sheep and cattle, and the money changers had set up their tables within this sacred court.

Jesus was angry. All this clamour of voices, lowing of cattle, and bleating of sheep, broke the peace of God's house and disturbed the earnest and weary men and women who had come to worship God. He smote the buyers and the sellers, and He drove out the money-changers. The sheep and the oxen were hurried out of the temple court. But, as we might expect, He did not touch the doves in their baskets. He said to those who were selling doves, " Take these things hence ; make not My Father's house an house of merchandise."

Soon the temple court was cleared, and a new quietness fell upon the place. The disciples of Jesus looked at Him with a new amazement, and they understood why He had been so angry. They saw that He had fulfilled an old prophecy, " The zeal of Thine house hath eaten me up."

THE WOMAN AT THE WELL

When Jesus went up every year to the feast of the Passover He came back to Galilee by one of the two roads from Jerusalem. One was the low road along the bank of the Jordan. The other was the high road that led through the hills of Palestine. It was a hard and stony track, and there were many dangers to be faced, especially of robbers, who watched for lonely travellers. But worst of all, it ran through Samaria, and the Jews and the Samaritans hated each other, so that they were rude to each other. A Samaritan would not give a night's lodging to a Jew. But Jesus made up His mind to take this hard and unpleasant road, for He had a kind purpose in His heart.

On the second day of His journey, at midday, He came near to a village called Sychar. He rested at a famous well, which had been dug long ago by Jacob, about a mile from the village. It was the month of April, and the day was hot. Jesus was weary with His journey, and He was both hungry and thirsty.

So He sat down to rest Himself on the edge of the well, while the disciples went into the village to buy bread.

As He was sitting there, a woman came, alone, to draw water from the well. He rose up and said, " Give Me to drink." She turned to look at Him, with a hard and stony stare, and she said, " How is it that Thou, being a Jew, askest drink of me, which am a woman of Samaria ? "

Jesus was sorry for her. He saw that she needed not only this water from Jacob's well, but water from the well of God's goodness, to satisfy the thirst of her soul, and to cleanse her heart. So He said, " If thou knewest the gift of God, and who it is that saith to thee, Give Me to drink ; thou wouldst have asked of Him, and He would have given thee living water." The woman said to Him, " Sir, Thou hast nothing to draw with, and the well is deep : from whence then hast Thou that living water ? " But Jesus said to her very gently, " Whosoever drinketh of the water that I shall give him shall never thirst."

Now this woman of Samaria was a poor outcast, with whom other women would not keep company. She was living a sinful life, and that was why she came to the well at midday and alone. But Jesus looked at her with a great pity in His heart. He wanted to bring her back to God and to live a pure and holy life, so He said to her, " Go, call thy husband, and come hither."

The woman was amazed, and flushed with shame.

How did this stranger know about her life and her home? She answered in low tones, "I have no husband." Jesus told her that He knew she had no husband, and that she was living a wicked life. The woman did not want anything more said about her life. So she began to speak about the bitter quarrel between the Jews and the Samaritans. The Jews said that the temple at Jerusalem was the only place where God could be worshipped. The Samaritans said that God could be worshipped on their mountain, and that they need not go to Jerusalem. Jesus replied, "Woman, believe Me, the hour cometh when ye shall, neither in this mountain, nor yet at Jerusalem, worship the Father." He meant to tell her that God could be worshipped anywhere, because He was the Father of all men. Then He said, " God is a spirit, and they that worship Him must worship Him in spirit and in truth."

As He said these words the woman looked at Him intently, and with a new wonder. She saw how wise He was, and she felt herself to be ignorant. So she said that when Christ would come He would make people wise about all these things. Then said Jesus, " I, that speak unto thee, am the Christ."

As He said this the disciples came back from the village with the bread they had bought. They marvelled to see Jesus speaking with a woman, and with such a woman as this outcast of Sychar. They said nothing, but their looks showed what they thought. But the woman had been changed in heart. She had begun to see how impure her life was, and how far she was from God. She forgot all about the water, and left her water-pot lying by the well, and hastened into the city to tell the men she knew about her wonderful talk with Jesus. She said to them, " Come, see a man which told me all things that ever I did : is not this the Christ ? "

Now Jesus was deeply moved in His spirit. He sat very still, with His face shining with joy. The disciples prepared the meal, and sat down beside Him. But Jesus did not eat. So they prayed Him, saying, " Master, eat." They spoke quietly one to another, wondering if any one had brought Him something to eat while they were away. But Jesus said, " I have meat to eat that ye know not of. My meat is to do the will of Him that sent Me, and to finish His work." By this He meant to tell them of the rapture He had in the changed heart of the woman of Samaria.

The whole city of Samaria wondered when they saw the change in the woman who had gone out to the well. They knew that she had been living a sinful life. Now, she went about among them, pure and gentle, humble and kind. Some of the people who saw her, and heard her tell her story, also believed in Jesus. They went out to the well, and besought Him to come with them into the city, and stay a little while. So Jesus and His disciples went with them, and spent two days speaking to them of His Father in Heaven, who loved all men, both Jews and Samaritans.

The Stilling of the Storm

After Jesus had made the water into wine at Cana in Galilee, and had cleansed the temple at Jerusalem, His name was on every one's lips. He left Nazareth and went down to live in Capernaum, and there He stayed so long a time, and did so many wonderful works, that it was known as "His own city."

He began by preaching in the synagogue in Capernaum on the Sabbath days. But there was not room enough to hold the crowds who came to its door. So He led them down to the shore of the lake, and getting into Peter's boat He stood in the stern, and spoke to the people who stood on the shore.

But Jesus began to feel that His strength was failing. He felt that He must depart to some quiet place, and find rest. So after a long day's preaching, in which He taught the people many parables, He sent them away. It was the evening hour, and He called His disciples and said to them, "Let us pass over to the other side," for the other side of the lake was a quiet and lonely region.

Jesus was quite tired out, so He went to the stern of the boat, and lay down to rest. The disciples brought Him the steersman's leather cushion for His pillow. He laid his head upon it, and soon was fast asleep.

The Sea of Galilee is a large lake about thirteen miles long by seven miles broad. It lies deep down in the valley of the Jordan, with high hills rising on both sides. That evening, when the boat which carried Jesus and the other little ships along with it were crossing the lake, just as the darkness came on, a terrible storm burst over the waters. The waves rose higher and higher, and began to break over the boat, until the disciples feared that she would sink, and they would all be drowned.

But Jesus was so weary in body and so calm in spirit, that He slept on, untroubled by the driving of the storm and the lashing of the waves. The disciples looked at Him in astonishment, but did not care to wake Him. At last their terror became too great, and they went to Him and cried, " Master, carest Thou not that we perish ? "

Jesus opened His eyes and looked calmly up at the black heavens, and listened to the terrific howling of the winds. He seemed quite unmoved. But when He saw the fearful and despairing looks of His disciples, He arose, and in a quiet, clear voice he checked the wind, and He said to the waves, " Peace, be still." The wind fell away, the tossing waters sank into quietness, and there was a great calm. As a Christian poet has written,—

> " The winds were howling o'er the deep,
>   Each wave a watery hill ;
>   The Saviour wakened from His sleep ;
>   He spake, and all was still."

Then He turned to the disciples and said to them, " Why are ye so fearful ? How is it that ye have no faith?" He stilled the storm because He was sorry for the terrified disciples. He slept on because He knew Himself to be like a child in His Father's arms. What He wanted always was that men should have no fear in any storm, but should have faith in God's goodness and care.

The disciples were astonished, and looked at Jesus with new and adoring eyes. They began to speak to each other and to say, "What manner of man is this, that even the wind and the sea obey Him?"

THE GRACE OF THE LORD JESUS

THE WOMAN WHO WAS A SINNER

WHEN Jesus began to go through the land preaching the good news of God, the plain and simple folk heard Him gladly. As He continued His wonderful ministry, and showed His compassion not only for the sick and the sorrowing, but for the sinful men and women among the people, many of the outcasts began to follow Him. They repented of their sins, and lived changed lives, and some of them became His disciples. Because He was so eager to bring these poor sinners to God He was called "the friend of publicans and sinners."

Now there was a man named Simon, who was one of the Pharisees. The Pharisees believed themselves to be God's favoured servants. But some of them were proud and vain, and others were covetous and insincere. There were some who were good men, but they were not willing to believe that Jesus was God's Son, and the promised Saviour, and no one of them became His disciple. Simon lived in Magdala, a fishing town on the Sea of Galilee. When Jesus paid a visit to Magdala, Simon heard of His coming, and invited Him to a feast in his house.

Now Simon, the Pharisee, thought that he was

doing Jesus a great favour and paying Him much honour in asking Him to sit at his table. He had heard of Jesus as the simple and unlearned carpenter of Nazareth. So he did not trouble to show Him any of the marks of honour which were usually shown to his guests. In the East the giver of a feast welcomes his guests with a kiss. He bids his servant unloose their sandals, and bathe their feet by pouring on water, and drying them with a towel. He shows them a special mark of respect by pouring cool, sweet-smelling ointment on their head. Simon paid Jesus none of these courteous attentions. But Jesus took no notice of this slight. He sat down quietly in the place given to Him.

The guests at such a feast did not sit on chairs as we do. Each was given a couch, with its head drawn up to the table, on which he reclined. The doors of an Eastern house are left open, so that any one can pass out and in. So when the supper was beginning a woman came in. She had an alabaster vase filled with precious ointment, and she meant to pour it on the head of Jesus. But when she saw Him, and noticed that His feet had not been washed, and when she thought of His kindness and compassion, she stood still. Great tears fell from her eyes upon His feet as she stooped to kneel behind Him. She was vexed and ashamed, but she took her long hair, which hung over her shoulders, and wiped away the tears. Then she imprinted a kiss on His feet, and poured the ointment over them.

Now this woman was one of those poor sinners whom Jesus pitied, and whom He had brought to repent of her sins. Simon the Pharisee looked on with amazement, almost with horror, as she drew near to Jesus and wiped His feet with her hair and kissed them. He would not have allowed such a woman to come near him. He said nothing, but he thought to himself that Jesus could not be a prophet, or He would have known what manner of woman this was which had touched Him, and He would have bidden her to leave the room.

Jesus knew his thoughts, and He spoke this little parable, " There was a certain man which had two debtors : the one owed five hundred pence, and the other fifty. And when they had nothing to pay, he frankly forgave them both. Tell me, therefore, which of them will love him most ? " Simon at once answered, " I suppose that he to whom he forgave most."

Then Jesus looked toward the woman, and He reminded Simon that he had given Him no water to wash His feet, no kiss of welcome, no ointment on His head. But this woman had lavished upon Him not only her ointment, but her kiss and her tears.

Then He went on to say, looking at Simon with eyes before whose gaze Simon must have been ashamed, " To whom little is forgiven, the same loveth little." He meant to say that if Simon would repent of his sins, which were many more than he knew, and if he were forgiven them, he would love God and men more than he did, and would lavish kindness and courtesy upon them.

The poor woman stood by while Jesus was speaking, greatly wondering. She felt keenly that Simon the Pharisee had looked at her with his hard and contemptuous eyes. So Jesus said at once, " Thy sins are forgiven," and then He added, " Thy faith hath saved thee, go in peace."

The Ruler's Daughter

We are often told in the story of the life of Jesus that He was moved with compassion. That means that His loving and tender heart was full of pity, and He was eager with desire to heal and to comfort and to help. That is the grace of the Lord Jesus, for all things of grace are gentle and kind and lovely.

One day He crossed the Sea of Galilee from its opposite side. When He came out of the boat, a ruler of the synagogue named Jairus came to meet Him. He had only one child, a little daughter, twelve years old. She fell sick, and the ruler and his wife had watched beside her bed for some days. Now they had lost hope, and she lay dying. But He remembered Jesus, and he came to Him, and he fell down at His feet, and cried earnestly, " My little daughter lieth at the point of death : come, and lay Thy hands on her, that she may be healed ; and she shall live."

Now among the crowd that thronged Jesus there was a woman who had suffered from a wasting disease for twelve years. She had heard of Jesus, and of His healing of the sick, and she believed He would heal her if only she could get near to Him. She said to herself, " If I may touch but His clothes, I

A Street in the East.

shall be whole." So she crept in behind Him, stretched out her hand, and touched the hem of His garment, and at once she was healed.

The poor woman thought that Jesus would not know, for she touched very gently. She intended to slip quietly away with a deep gratefulness in her heart. But Jesus knew the difference between the jostling of the crowd and this appealing touch of the woman in her need. So He turned round, and He asked, " Who touched My clothes ? " for He knew that healing virtue had gone out of Him to some one. The disciples said to Him that it was strange for Him to ask, " Who touched Me ? " when He was being thronged on every side. But the woman, trembling and fearing lest Jesus should think that she had taken a liberty, fell down before Him and told Him all her story. Jesus looked at her with one of His kind expressions, and said, very gently, " Daughter, thy faith hath made thee whole : go in peace and be whole of thy plague."

All this time Jairus had been waiting with anguish. He had left his little daughter at the point of death, and now he began to think that it was too late, and that they would find her dead, when they came to his house. And at that moment a message came to him, " Thy daughter is dead ; why troublest thou the Master any further ? "

At once Jesus turned to Jairus, and said to him, " Be not afraid, only believe." He would not be longer delayed by the crowd. So He took with Him only Peter and James and John, and He hastened with Jairus to his home. When they came to the house they heard the tumult made by the neighbours, and the wailing and shrieking of the women who mourned. He hushed the noise, and put them out of the house, and said, " Why make ye this ado and weep ? the damsel is not dead, but sleepeth."

Then Jesus, taking with Him the little girl's father

and mother, and Peter and James and John, went
into the room where the little girl was lying, white
and still.   He took her cold hand in His and He said,
" Talitha Cumi," that is to say, " Little one, arise."
At once she opened her eyes, and looked at them all.
All the people were astonished, but Jairus and his
wife were filled with a deep gratitude, and they saw
the grace of the Lord Jesus.

SEEKING THE LOST

As time went on some of those who had begun to
follow Jesus left Him.   They were not willing to give
up all, to become His disciples.   But the tax-gatherers
and the sinners who were scorned and despised, and
cast out of the synagogue, drew near to listen to
Him.

One of these tax-gatherers, named Matthew, who
had left all and risen up from his seat, where he
gathered the people's money, to become one of His
disciples, made a feast for Jesus.   He invited a great
many of the poor sinful folk to sit down in his house.
Another tax-gatherer had also gathered a company
together, and Jesus went in to supper with him.
The Pharisees were shocked, and went about murmuring, with bitterness, " This Man receiveth sinners,
and eateth with them."   They thought that Jesus
showed that He was not a teacher sent from God
when He kept such evil company.   Jesus heard of
their murmuring, and so He told three most beautiful

stories to explain why He companied with publicans and sinners, and sat down with joy at their feasts.

The first was the story of a shepherd who kept his flock on the high, bare hill-side. He had a hundred sheep, and he knew them all by their names. When he called them together one evening to lead them home to the fold, he found that only ninety and nine answered his call. One was amissing. He left the ninety and nine just where they were, although it was the wilderness, and went out to seek that one lost sheep, until he found it. It had strayed far away, and was now tired and trembling with fear. So he took it up and carried it back on his shoulder with great joy.

The second was the story of a woman who had ten pieces of silver. She lost one of them and was much concerned. She lighted the lamp, and began to sweep the whole house, with keen glances into every corner. At last she found her lost coin. Then she called her friends and neighbours together to rejoice with her, because she had found the piece of silver which had been lost.

The third was the story of a father who had two sons. The younger son was tired of the quiet life at home. He wanted to see the world, and to take part in its excitement, and to share in its pleasures. So he asked his father to give him the portion of the goods which would fall to him after his father's death. His father gave him the money, and he set out for a far country, and there he wasted what had been given him in reckless, evil ways.

But when he had squandered it all, he began to be in want. He asked a farmer to allow him to work for him at the meanest and vilest work of all. That was to feed the swine in the fields. He was brought so low, that he had to satisfy his hunger by eating the husks with which he fed the swine.

As he sat by the swine troughs, hungry and miserable and ashamed, he began to think about his father, and his father's home. He remembered that even the servants in his father's house had enough to eat and to spare, while he was perishing with hunger. So he said to himself, " I will arise and go to my father, and will say unto him, Father, I have sinned against heaven and before thee and am no more worthy to be called thy son : make me as one of thy hired servants."

So he arose, and set out on his long journey home. His father had always sorrowed for his lost son, and longed to see his face again. He had often looked along the road, in the hope that he would catch sight of him returning home. One day his eyes were gladdened, as he saw, a great way off, his prodigal son on the way to the house. He was full of compassion, and he ran and fell upon his neck, and kissed him.

His son looked up into his face with shame, and he said, " Father, I have sinned against heaven, and in thy sight, and am no more worthy to be called thy son." He had intended to repeat all he had said when he was sitting by the swine troughs, but his father broke in, " Bring forth the best robe and put it on him ; and put a ring on his hand, and shoes on his feet : and bring hither the fatted calf and kill it ; and let us eat and be merry ; for this my son was dead and is alive again ; he was lost and is found." No one, not even of the Pharisees, could miss Christ's meaning. As the father longed after his lost son, so God longs after His lost children, and is always seeking them. And when they come back to Him and to His house, He is filled with joy, and bids them sit down at His table. That was why Jesus received sinners, and sat down to eat with them, when they had come back to God.

WHO IS MY NEIGHBOUR ?

Jesus, who came to be the Saviour and the King of the Jews, loved them with all His heart. They were His own people, and He often sorrowed that they would not hear His message, and He wept over Jerusalem when He foresaw that that city and its temple would be destroyed. But they were angry with Him, and their leaders and teachers were offended when they saw the people listening so eagerly to Him.

He was teaching in a synagogue on the Sabbath day, and He was speaking to the people about eternal life. Sitting in the synagogue that day there was a teacher of the law. He was a learned man, who knew the Scriptures, and he thought that he would put a difficult question to Jesus, and would puzzle Him before the people, and lead Him on to an argument in which He might be put to confusion.

So he stood up, and asked Jesus, " Master, what shall I do to inherit eternal life ? " Jesus knew that he was a teacher of the law, and He answered, " What is written in the law ? how readest thou ? " The lawyer replied, " Thou shalt love the Lord thy God with all thy heart, and with all thy soul, and with all thy strength, and with all thy mind ; and thy neighbour as thyself." Then Jesus said to him, " Thou hast answered right : this do, and thou shalt have eternal life."

The people saw that Jesus had answered this lawyer out of His own mouth. But the lawyer thought that he saw how he could catch Jesus, and lead him on to an argument. So he said, " And who is my neighbour ? "

Jesus would not enter upon any debate or argument in the synagogue, but He told the people this story. He said that a certain man went down from Jerusalem to Jericho. That road is a long and steep and lonely path, and it is haunted by robbers. As this man was passing along he came to a lonely place, when a number of thieves rushed out upon him, stripped him of his raiment, and cruelly wounded him, and left him by the side of the road half dead.

As he lay there moaning and in great pain, a priest from the temple at Jerusalem came down the hill. He saw the man, and marked how ill he was, and how naked, and how bleeding with wounds, but he did not want to trouble himself, as he was in a hurry to get to Jericho. So he took the other side of the road, and passed on his way.

A short time afterwards a Levite, who was one of the attendants at the temple services, came to the place where the poor man was lying. He looked at him and saw how much need he had of help. But he was not willing to trouble himself, and so he passed by on the other side.

Then there came a Samaritan, who was journeying on his business, and when he saw the wounded man, he was full of pity for him. He went to him and saw him lying almost unclothed, and he marked his painful wounds. He poured in oil and wine so as to lessen the pain. He lifted him up upon his beast, and walking by his side, he took him down the hill to the inn. That night he took care of him, and watched over him, the whole night long. Early next morning, when this good Samaritan departed, because he had to attend to his business, he went to the landlord of the inn, and took out some money, and said, " Take care of him ; and whatsoever thou spendest more, when I come again I will repay thee."

Then Jesus looked to the lawyer and He asked him, " Which now of these three, thinkest thou, was neighbour unto him that fell among the thieves ? " The lawyer could make no answer but one, " He that showed mercy on him." Then said Jesus, " Go thou, and do likewise."

The Shining Face of Christ

As Jesus went through the towns and villages teaching and healing, the people began to wonder and to question about Him. The priests and the scribes, who were jealous of Him, would not pay Him any honour. The people said that never man spake as He did, and that no one did His wonderful works. But only His disciples began to be sure that He was the Son of God, and that He was Christ. So Jesus knew that the time had come when He would declare Himself to them.

There is a high range of hills in the north of Palestine called the Lebanon Mountains. At the foot of one of these hills there nestled the little village of Cæsarea Philippi. It was a place of wonderful beauty, with many clear, cool streams, and pleasant walks among the woods. To this village Jesus led His disciples. There they held long conversations on the love of God to His people, and they spent hours in meditation and prayer.

One day as they went out to walk together, He came to a quiet spot in the woods, and He sat down and gathered His disciples around Him. He put to them the question over which He had been brooding, " Whom do men say that I am ? " They told Him that some said He was John the Baptist. Others said that He was Elias, and others that He was Jeremias, or some other of the prophets. He paused for a moment, and then said, " But whom do ye say that I am ? " The sudden question stilled them all. until Peter, with deep feeling, cried, " Thou art the Christ, the Son of the Living God."

Now this was an hour for which Jesus had waited, and for which He had longed. So when Peter made this great confession, the heart of Jesus throbbed with joy, and His face was kindled into brightness, and He said to Peter, " Blessed art thou, Simon, son of Jonas : for flesh and blood hath not revealed it unto thee, but My Father which is in heaven." But He forbade them to tell any one, for He knew that if His enemies heard Him proclaimed as Christ, they would be filled with rage, and they would rouse the people against Him.

Six days passed away in this quiet retreat, and then the disciples saw the shining face of Jesus again. Taking Peter and James and John with Him, for they were the most trusted and the most beloved of His disciples, He climbed one of the hills to find a place where they could be quite alone. So, in the quietness of the mountain top, He began to pray, and like all who pray much, His face grew beautiful, and it began to glow with a wonderful sheen of brightness. This brightness increased until He was wholly transfigured. " His face did shine as the sun, and His raiment was white as the light."

While they were looking on at this great sight, they had a vision which bewildered them. In that vision they saw Moses and Elias talking with Jesus. The

"*Little one, arise.*"

"He passed in to find the streets crowded with an excited multitude."

(See page 180)

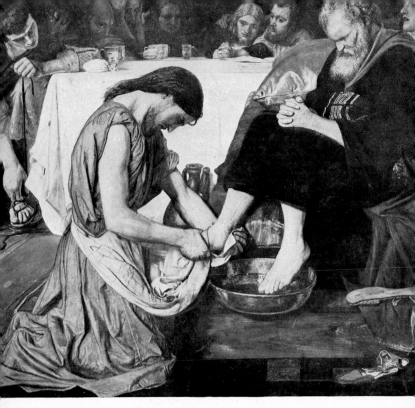

He began to wash his feet.

(See page 185)

disciples felt that this mountain top was holy ground. Peter said to Jesus, " Lord, it is good for us to be here ; if Thou wilt, let us make here three tabernacles : one for Thee, and one for Moses, and one for Elias."

As he was speaking a bright cloud came down and hid Jesus and Moses and Elias from them. Then a voice called out of the cloud, " This is My beloved Son, in whom I am well pleased : hear ye Him."

They came down from the mountain to join the other disciples. Jesus charged them not to tell them of what they had seen on the mountain top, and He gave them His reason for keeping it a secret. He told them that He would soon suffer a cruel death on the cross at Jerusalem. So when Peter, James, and John came to the other disciples, they did not speak of the glory of the shining face of Jesus, which they had seen on the mount. Neither did they tell them of what Jesus had said of His sufferings, and of His death, and of His rising from the dead. But in after days they remembered His words.

THE DAYS OF SORROW

THE TRIUMPHAL ENTRY INTO JERUSALEM

WHEN the time of the Passover drew near
Jesus went up, along with His disciples, to
Jerusalem. On the way He took them
aside, and told them the burden of His spirit.
" Behold, we go up to Jerusalem, and the Son of
Man shall be betrayed unto the chief priests and unto
the scribes, and they shall condemn Him to death."

He travelled towards Jerusalem, by the steep road
from the Jordan, and He drew near to a village called
Bethphage, where He had a friend. He was very
weary with His journey, so He sent His disciples
into the village, saying to them, that they would
find, at the cross roads, an ass tied, and by her side
a colt.

When the disciples came back with the colt they
spread some of their clothes on his back, and they set
Jesus on him, and went forward to the city.

A great multitude streamed out of the city, and met
Jesus on His way. They took their garments, and
they cut down green branches from the trees, and
strewed them on the road, for that was the fashion
of receiving a king. So Jesus rode on in the midst
of a multitude of people who were filled with joy,

and were shouting "Hosanna! blessed is He that cometh in the name of the Lord; Hosanna in the Highest!"

When Jesus reached the summit of the Mount of Olives, He came in sight of Jerusalem. The city lies across a deep valley, and it stood out before Him, as though it were at His feet.

The Damascus Gate, Jerusalem.

He stopped the procession. A silence fell upon the multitude. The tears came to His eyes, and He wept, and He said, "The day shall come upon thee that they shall not leave in thee one stone upon another; because thou knewest not the time of thy visitation." He meant to tell them of the doom of the city, because they would not receive Him as their Lord.

Then He passed on down the deep descent to the bridge over the brook Kidron, and He went up by the way that led to the city gate. He passed in to find the streets crowded with an excited multitude, some of whom were strangers who had come to the feast. They were asking the question, " Who is this ? " and the people replied, " This is Jesus, the prophet of Nazareth of Galilee."

Jesus entered Jerusalem and rode straight to the gate of the temple court. He passed inside and stood among the people in perfect silence. He looked round about Him and saw all that was going on. He knew that this was God's house, and should be holy, and He remembered that day when He was a boy of twelve years of age, and found it to be God's house to Him.

As He was standing, many little children who had been among the multitude, and had caught up the words of welcome given to Jesus, broke into singing, " Hosanna to the Son of David." Jesus loved the voices of little children, and He was gladdened by hearing them sing, in the temple court. The priests were angry, and they said that Jesus should rebuke these children, and hush their songs. Jesus answered, " Have ye never read, Out of the mouths of babes and sucklings thou hast perfect praise ? "

The Home in Bethany

In the village of Bethany, about two miles from Jerusalem, there lived a dear friend of Jesus, named Lazarus, with his two sisters, Martha and Mary. They all loved Jesus, and always gladly welcomed Him to their home.

Martha was eager to show Him much honour. So she set about preparing a supper. She spared no pains, and she bustled through the house preparing the meal. But Mary hungered to hear Jesus speak of the Father in Heaven and His love, and she sat down near Jesus to listen to His words, with wondering eyes. When she saw Mary sitting so quietly, she went to Jesus and asked Him, " Lord, dost Thou not care that my sister hath left me to serve alone ? bid her, therefore, that she help me."

Jesus was vexed at her words, but He answered her very gently, " Martha, Martha, thou art careful and troubled about many things : but one thing is needful." Then He said that Mary, who sat down to make Him glad with her love and her fellowship, was choosing a better way than Martha had done, with all her over-anxious service.

Some time afterwards a heavy sorrow fell on this home in Bethany. Lazarus was sick, and his sisters began to fear that he would die. They sent a message to Jesus to tell Him how ill His friend was. They expected that He would come at once to see Lazarus, but Jesus stayed two days where He was. That

seemed strange to His disciples, but Jesus meant to
show both His love for Lazarus, and His power to
overcome death and its sorrow.

Before Jesus reached Bethany, Lazarus had been
four days in the grave. When Martha heard that
Jesus was coming she went out to meet Him, but
Mary sat still in the house. Martha looked at Jesus
with some reproach, and said, " Lord, if Thou hadst
been here, my brother had not died." Jesus said
unto her, " Thy brother shall rise again."

When Jesus saw the deep grief in which Martha and
Mary and all their friends were cast, He was greatly
troubled, and He asked them to show Him the grave
of Lazarus. As He went to the place, He wept with
them. The grave was a cave, and a stone covered
the mouth of the grave. Jesus said to the people,
" Take ye away the stone."

Then Jesus lifted up His eyes, and prayed, " Father,
I thank Thee that Thou hast heard Me. And I knew
that Thou hearest Me always." After He had prayed,
He cried with a loud voice, " Lazarus, come forth."
To the wonder of all, Lazarus rose up, and came
forth, with the grave-clothes wrapped around him,
and his face bound with a napkin. Jesus said to them,
" Loose him, and let him go." The home in Bethany
was a place of joy when Martha and Mary received
Lazarus, risen from the dead.

When Jesus came up to His last Passover, the
family in Bethany showed Him many kindnesses.
Martha invited Him and all His disciples one evening

to a supper. When the feast had begun, Mary remembered that one of the special marks of love and honour to a guest was to pour a sweet-smelling oil on his head. She slipped away to her room, where she kept an alabaster vase filled with a costly ointment. She came back and broke the seal, and poured it upon the head of Jesus, and the whole house was filled with its fragrant odour.

This was so costly an offering, that even the disciples began to think that Mary had done a foolish thing and that it was waste, to pour it all on the head of Jesus. One of them said that it might have been sold for three hundred pence, and the money might have been given to the poor. But Jesus said, " Let her alone ; why trouble ye her ? she hath done a beautiful thing to Me. For ye have the poor with you always, and whensoever ye will, ye may do them good ; but Me ye have not always."

Jesus knew that in a few days He would be crucified, and be laid in the tomb. He remembered that it was the custom of sorrowing friends to pour such sweet-smelling ointment upon the body of the dead. So He told the company that Mary, whether she meant it or not, had been doing what love always did, for those who were being buried. Then, looking round upon them all, he said, " Wheresoever this gospel shall be preached throughout the whole world, this also that she hath done, shall be spoken of for a memorial of her." Mary's deed of love will never be forgotten.

The Upper Room and its Supper

Jesus spent every day, except one, of the week of His last Passover in the temple, teaching the people. Each evening He went out of the city and passed the night, sometimes in a friend's house, and sometimes in the shelter of the woods.

He had a friend in Jerusalem who was willing and eager to serve Him in any way. We do not know his name, for he is always spoken of as " the goodman of the house." He had a house in the city, with many rooms, and with one large upper room, well furnished, so as to receive guests. Two days before the night on which the Jews used to hold the Feast of the Passover, and to sacrifice the lamb, the disciples asked Jesus, " Where wilt Thou that we go and prepare, that Thou mayest eat the Passover ? "

Jesus, of course, had been thinking about this. So He sent two disciples to Jerusalem, and said to them, " Go ye into the city, and there shall meet you a man bearing a pitcher of water ; follow him. And wheresoever he shall go in, say ye to the goodman of the house, The Master saith, Where is the guest-chamber where I shall eat the Passover with My disciples ? " The goodman, as soon as he heard the message of Jesus, showed them the upper room, all ready for the supper.

So in the evening they went in together, and sat around the table in the upper room. Jesus saw that they all had sat down, after walking in to the city along the dusty country road, without having washed their feet. But as the disciples had come along the road they had been disputing which of them should be the greatest in the kingdom, and who should hold the chief place of honour. They were in a sulky and sullen mood, and no one of them would humble himself, to wash the feet of any one of his fellow-disciples.

Jesus was grieved. He took a towel, and poured water into a basin, and stooping down behind Simon Peter, He began to wash his feet. Peter was ashamed, and he cried, " Lord, dost Thou wash my feet ? Thou shalt never wash my feet." Jesus said to him, " If I wash thee not, thou hast no part with Me." When He had washed Peter's feet He went round the whole company, one by one, washing even the feet of Judas Iscariot, who was about to betray Him. Then He put on His robe again, and sat down at the table, and He asked them, " Know ye what I have done to you ? "

Jesus knew that they thought He had washed their feet only to rebuke them. So Jesus said to them, " Ye call Me Master and Lord ; and ye say well, for so I am. If I, then, your Lord and Master, have washed your feet ; ye also ought to wash one another's feet. For I have given you an example that ye should do as I have done to you." Whenever we begin to be proud and high-minded, and will not take our share in the simple and lowly services of life, we are forgetting the example of Jesus, who stooped to wash His disciples' feet.

As the supper went on, Jesus sat in silence, and the disciples saw that He was exceedingly sad. He looked round about upon them all, and said, " Verily, I say unto you, one of you, which eateth with Me, shall betray Me." At this they were amazed and vexed, and began to say to Him one by one, " Is it I ? " " Is it I ? " Jesus answered, " It is one of the twelve that dippeth with Me in the dish. Woe to that man by whom the Son of Man is betrayed ! good were it for that man if he had never been born." The disciple He meant, although the others did not know, was Judas Iscariot.

The supper drew to a close. But before rising from the table Jesus turned it into that celebration and sacrament which all who love Him continue to observe. He took a piece of bread, and He offered a thanksgiving to God. Then He broke it, and passed it round the company, and each of them took a little bit from it, and ate it, while Jesus said, " Take, eat ; this is My body ; which is broken for you." Then He took the cup of wine, and again He offered a prayer of thanksgiving, and as it was passed round, they all drank of it, while Jesus said, " This is my blood of the new covenant, which is shed for many, for the remission of sins."

These were words so strange to them that they did not understand them. Only when Jesus died and rose again from the dead, did they understand why He had gathered them in the upper room of the goodman's house, and why He gave them this feast, with His command to observe it, in remembrance of Him, and of His love and death.

The Garden of Gethsemane

After they had sung a hymn, Jesus and His disciples left the upper room and went out to pass the night in the woods on the slope of the Mount of Olives. Jesus was sad and downcast, and He walked on for a little while without speaking. Then He said to the disciples, "All ye shall be offended because of Me this night ; for it is written, I will smite the shepherd, and the sheep shall be scattered."

They came to a garden named Gethsemane, and found a place of shelter among its olive trees. But He took Peter and James and John with Him, and went a little farther into the olive grove. As they were walking on, He said to the three disciples, " My soul is exceeding sorrowful even unto death : tarry ye here, and watch." He left them and went a little farther, and fell on His face, and prayed, " Father, all things are possible unto Thee ; take away this cup from Me ; nevertheless not what I will, but what Thou wilt." When He came back to the three disciples He found them asleep. He knew how tired and how sorrowful they were, so He left them asleep, and went back to His lonely spot, and prayed again, " Not My will, but Thine be done."

So He came back, calm and composed, and said to the disciples, " Sleep on now, and take your rest ; the hour is come ; behold, the Son of Man is betrayed into the hands of sinners. Rise up, let us go ; lo, he that betrayeth Me is at hand."

Judas Iscariot had left the upper room before the end of the feast. He resolved to desert Jesus. So he went, secretly, to the chief priests, and told them that he would lead them to the place where Jesus was passing the night. They were delighted, and promised to give him thirty pieces of silver as a reward. He gave them a sign by which they would know Jesus from any disciple, for when they found Him in the garden he would kiss Him.

Then the high priest called a number of his servants and armed them with swords and staves, and Judas led them out to the garden of Gethsemane.

Then Judas went up to Jesus, and said, " Hail, Master," and kissed Him, and Jesus, with a look of reproach Judas never forgot, said to him, " Betrayest thou the Son of Man with a kiss ? "

Jesus turned to the officers of the chief priests, and said to them, "Are ye come out, as against a thief, with swords and staves for to take Me ? I sat daily with you teaching in the temple, and ye laid no hold on Me." But they paid no heed to the words of Jesus, but laid hands upon Him, and took Him away.

Judas and the band of men took Jesus to the high priest's palace. It was past midnight, but the high priest had gathered a large company of priests and

scribes to try Jesus. They called witnesses to give
evidence against Him, but no one could tell of anything He had done, for which He should be punished.
Then they began to question Him, and when the high
priest asked Him, " Art Thou the Christ, the Son of
the Blessed ? " Jesus said, " I am." The high priest
rent his clothes, to show how much he was shocked,
and said that Jesus was a blasphemer against God,
and He must be put to death. He gave Him over to
his band of servants, and they mocked Him, and
spat upon Him, and smote Him with their hands.
Jesus bore it meekly, and in silence.

Now Peter, who had fled out of the garden along
with the other disciples, came back to the road, and
followed the band who had seized Jesus, keeping a
good long way behind them. He wanted to see what
would happen to Jesus. He went into the court of
the priest's palace, and sat down at the fire where the
high priest's high servants were warming themselves.
He thought that no one would recognise him as one of
the disciples of Jesus. But one of the maids of the
high priest noticed him, and she said, " Thou also wast
with Jesus of Nazareth." Peter denied it. Immediately
he heard a cock crow, and he remembered the words
of Jesus, when He said that before the cock would
crow, he would deny Him thrice. He lifted his eyes
and saw Jesus looking at him. He remembered all
Jesus had been to him, and how deeply Jesus loved
him. Shame broke his heart, and he fled out of the
court, weeping bitterly.

CHRIST BEFORE PILATE

The chief priests who condemned Jesus had no power to put Him to death. So they led Him, as soon as the morning light had come, to Pilate.

Pilate took his seat in his judgment hall, and Jesus was brought in before him. The chief priests made many charges against Him, as an evil-doer who was stirring up the people to revolt. But he was a Roman, and had a clear sense of justice. So as he looked at Jesus and beheld His wondrous face, always with that high look of godlike calm, and as he listened to the accusations of the priests, he saw that Jesus was not an evil-doer, and that He had done nothing worthy of death, but that He was hated and plotted against by the Jewish priests and scribes.

When he went out of the judgment hall, he found that a multitude had gathered in the court of the palace. He said to them, " I find in Jesus no fault ; but ye have a custom, that I should release unto you a prisoner at the Passover ; will ye, therefore, that I release unto you the King of the Jews ? " By this time the people of Jerusalem had turned against Jesus. When He entered the city riding on the colt, they were filled with delight, for they thought that now He was about to show Himself as a King who, like David, would establish a throne of pomp and power.

So when Pilate offered to release Jesus they cried

out, " Not this man, but Barabbas." Now Barabbas was not only a rebel, but a robber and a murderer, yet they chose him instead of Jesus.

But Pilate was still unwilling to crucify Christ. He saw how innocent of any wrong-doing His life had been. He saw how gentle and patient He was. And his wife, who had heard Jesus speak, sent him a message that she had had a terrible dream about Jesus, and she begged him to do no harm to One whom she believed to be a just man. So when Pilate came out to the people he began to reason with them. He asked them to tell him what evil He had done. But the chief priests stirred the people up to repeat their demand for the release of Barabbas. Then Pilate asked, " What will ye then that I shall do unto Him whom ye call the King of the Jews ? " They cried out again, " Crucify Him, crucify Him."

Yet Pilate made one more effort to do Jesus justice. He went back to the judgment hall to speak to Jesus privately, and to find out who He really was. But Jesus made no reply to any of his questions.

Pilate was surprised that Jesus would not answer his questions, and he said to Him, " Knowest Thou not that I have power to crucify Thee, and have power to release Thee." Jesus looked at Pilate and said, in words that touched him to the quick, " Thou couldest have no power at all against Me, except it were given thee from above." So Pilate released Barabbas, and delivered Jesus to the soldiers to be scourged, as the custom was, before He was crucified.

They lashed Jesus until His back was torn and bleeding.

Then Pilate brought Him out to the people, in the hope that they would look on Him with compassion, and see that so holy a sufferer should not be put to death on the cross. As he brought Jesus before them, he cried aloud, " Behold the Man ! " But by this time their passion of anger was burning hot, and they cried, "Away with Him, away with Him ; crucify Him, crucify Him."

So Jesus was delivered up to the soldiers. They took Him back to the court of the palace, and began to mock and torment Him. They put on Him an old purple robe, because purple is the colour worn by kings. They platted a crown of thorns, and they put it on His head. They bowed down before Him, and cried in scornful mockery, " Hail, King of the Jews ! " After that they took off the robe, and put on His own plain garments, and made preparation to lead Him out to the Cross,

That is not the end of the story. Jesus would never again walk among men teaching and healing. This was the day of His death. But on the cross He would redeem the world, and He would make the cross His throne.

" Behold the Man ! "

(*See page* 192)

"Lord, lay not this sin to their charge."

THE RISEN SAVIOUR

Calvary and the Cross

WHEN the chief priests and rulers saw Jesus in the hands of the mocking and taunting soldiers they thought that all the story of his life and power and love was over. In a few hours, they felt sure, his body would be cast, along with the bodies of the two thieves who were crucified with Him, to some burning rubbish heap. That was what was done, in these cruel days with crucified evil-doers. Then His disciples would be scattered and would confess that they were mistaken, and had been deceived by Jesus. Soon, they said to each other, His name would be forgotten. They did not know that the word, Calvary, and the name for the most shameful method of death, the Cross, would become so dear to all men, that they would not be named except with mingled tears and songs.

Yet the day of Calvary and the Cross is the saddest of all the days of time. It was sad to Jesus. He was left alone. He was not only weary, but He was in pain. Only He knew that He was doing God's will. He was going in the way which His Father had marked out for Him. Yet, it was a dark and difficult way, and He felt the shadow of its loneliness falling upon His heart.

And it was a saddening day to many others. Mary, His mother, was not far away. Nothing will quench the love of a mother. She had friends who were sorrowing with her. Yet her pain of spirit was so great that she kept silence. There are times when words cannot be spoken. And it was a day of darkness to His disciples. They had forsaken Him when they saw Him in the hands of the soldiers. But they could not forget Him. One of them, the Apostle John, whom Jesus tenderly loved, did come to the cross to comfort Mary. Yet most of them had begun to think that Jesus had been mistaken, and that all He had told them was not to come to pass. " We thought it had been He which should have redeemed Israel," they said to each other. But their love still throbbed in their hearts, and the long hours of this day were dark and troubled.

Jesus had foreseen and foretold the sadness of this day : " Verily, verily, I say unto you, that ye shall weep and lament, but the world shall rejoice." But He knew that all this sadness would pass away, and that the whole world would be made glad by the story of Calvary and the Cross. " Ye shall be sorrowful, but your sorrow shall be turned into joy." In that light let us read the dark story with a new understanding.

Pilate, the Roman governor, had condemned Christ. But the chief priests and scribes gloated over their triumph. They had got rid of one who had become better loved by the people of the land than they were, and they had silenced the voice that had so often denounced their evil ways. They waited to see Jesus led out of Pilate's court by the soldiers, and some of them joined the crowd who were eager to see the spectacle of the crucifixion. They watched the soldiers laying two heavy beams on the shoulders of Jesus. These two beams were to form His cross, for the man who was about to be crucified always carried his cross to the place of his death.

It was not lawful to crucify any one inside the gates of the city. So the soldiers led Jesus out to a little hill called Calvary. Along with Him they led two thieves, who had been lying in prison awaiting their sentence of death. So, in the early forenoon, Jesus and the two thieves, guarded by the band of soldiers, passed through the streets of Jerusalem on their way to Calvary, and a great multitude of people accompanied them.

Jesus found that His strength was now quite exhausted. When we remember that He had been many hours without rest or food, and had been denied and betrayed, had stood before His judges, and been reviled by the people, and had been scourged and mocked by the soldiers, we do not wonder that He was quite unable to carry the two beams of His cross. The soldiers saw how worn He was, and they laid hold of a man named Simon, who belonged to Cyrene in Africa. He had come a long journey to take part in the Passover, and he was entering the city through the gate, when the soldiers seized him, and compelled him to carry Christ's cross. In after days he knew how high an honour had been paid him.

As the procession moved slowly on, some kind-hearted women, who had come out with their children, as working folk do when they go abroad, began to bewail and lament Jesus, when they saw Him going to be crucified. He was glad of their tender sympathy, and that made Him the more sorrowful as He foresaw the awful doom that would fall upon such women when Jerusalem was destroyed. He turned to them and said, " Daughters of Jerusalem, weep not for Me, but for yourselves and for your children." He knew that in those dreadful days when the Romans would assail the city, such simple folk would suffer horrible pains and die cruel deaths.

At last they came to the top of the hill. The soldiers took the wood and made the three crosses. On Christ's cross, and above His head, they fixed a superscription in large letters, that every one might read it, " Jesus of Nazareth, the King of the Jews." Then they fastened Jesus and the two thieves to their crosses, by driving great nails through their hands and their feet, and they raised them up and fixed them firmly in the ground.

The highway ran along near the place where Jesus was crucified. Some of the travellers passed along it with no more than a glance. Others who had heard of the wonderful works of Jesus, wagged their heads, and said, " He saved others, Himself He could not save." The rulers who had come out to see Him die uttered their bitter taunt, " He saved others ; let Him save Himself ; if He be Christ, the chosen of God." The soldiers, who heard these words of scorn, also began to mock, and they cried, " If Thou be the King of the Jews, save Thyself."

One of the two thieves who were crucified with Him began to rail upon Him. He had heard that Jesus had claimed to be Christ, so he said, " If Thou be the Christ, save Thyself and us." But the other had been watching Christ more closely. He had seen how gentle and how meek He was. He had heard Him pray, and he began to understand how wicked his own life had been, and to repent of his evil doings. So he looked towards Jesus, and said, " Lord, remember me, when Thou comest into Thy kingdom." Jesus was glad to hear one voice call Him " Lord " and to seek His blessing as He was dying on the cross.

Now the most wonderful thing in this story of the Cross of Jesus Christ was His unfailing faith in God, and His quenchless love to men. He never once complained, and He never said one hard word against any one. Even in the midst of His anguish, He took thought for others. There stood not very far from the cross, Mary, His mother, and her sister, and Mary Magdalene, and, with them, His beloved disciple, John. Jesus, looking at Mary, remembered all her love and care, and He knew that now she understood that strange saying of aged Simeon in the temple, that a sword should pierce her heart in the days to come. He saw that when He died she would have no one to care for her, and would have no home. So He said to her, and looked at John, " Woman, behold thy son." Then He said to John, " Behold thy mother." John understood what Jesus meant, and he took Mary to his own house.

Jesus hung upon the cross for three hours—from twelve o'clock to three o'clock in the afternoon. During those long three hours of agony He spoke seven times. Four of these sayings are full of tender meaning. In one of them He prayed for His murderers, saying, " Father, forgive them, for they know not what they do." In another, when His anguish, both of flesh and spirit, were extreme and even God, His Father, seemed not to care, He cried, " My God, My God, why hast Thou forsaken Me ? " Just as He was dying, He spoke a soft and quiet word of triumph, and He said, " It is finished." He knew that now He had finished the work God had given Him to do. Then He bowed His head, as He was about to die, and cried in a loud, clear voice, " Father, into Thy hands I commend My spirit."

The Jews who had been watching Jesus as he died remembered that the next day was the Sabbath. If the bodies of those who hung on the cross were not taken down before this day closed, they would hang all the next day in view of the people. They feared what might happen if the people came out to see that sight. They went to Pilate and besought him to command his soldiers to break the legs of Jesus and of the two thieves, so as to make sure that they were

dead, and then to bury them. The soldiers broke
the legs of the two thieves who still lingered on in
their agony. But they found that Jesus had already
died. We are glad to know that such cruel treat-
ment was not given to the body of Jesus.

At the foot of this hill called Calvary there was a
lovely garden. It belonged to a rich man, a Jewish
ruler, named Joseph of Arimathæa. He was a disciple
of Jesus, but he had not confessed his faith, for he was
afraid of the Jews. Now he came to Pilate and
begged to be given the body of Jesus that he might
give it fitting burial. He had a friend named Nicodemus, who was also a secret disciple of Jesus. He had
once come to Jesus by night, when no one would see
him, but he had never been brave enough to leave all
and follow Him. He brought a rich store of spices,
made of myrrh and aloes. These two took down the
body, anointed it with the sweet-smelling spices, and
wrapped it in a long cloth made of fine linen, clean
and white. There was in this garden a new tomb
which had been cut out of the rock. No one had yet
been buried in it. There, as the evening shadows
fell, and the flowers were closing for the night, they
laid the body of Jesus. When a great stone had been
rolled up to the mouth of the tomb, and laid upon it,
Joseph and Nicodemus left the garden in deep sorrow.

But the garden was not left in a lonely silence.
The Jews knew how deeply Jesus had been loved.
They began to fear that some of the disciples would
come, when it grew dark, and take away the body.

They went to Pilate and asked him to send a band of soldiers to keep guard beside the tomb. The night came on and passed, and the Sabbath day also came to a close. The soldiers kept their watch. But on the next night God sealed these soldiers' eyes in a deep sleep. They did not know of the coming of the angels. They did not hear the rolling away of the stone. Jesus arose from His grave in His glory, and passed by them, as they slept.

THE GLADDEST SUNDAY OF ALL TIME

WHEN Jesus died and was buried in the grave in Joseph's garden, the men and women who loved Him were filled with despair. The disciples were not only broken-hearted, but they were hopeless and ashamed. They were looked upon as men who might be openly mocked, because they had been deceived, and had been dreaming foolish dreams. Nothing seemed to be left for them, but to confess that they had been mistaken in Jesus, and then to go back to Galilee and to the life they had lived before He called them to follow Him. Suddenly their sorrow was turned into joy, for Jesus arose from the dead. The day of Christ's resurrection was the gladdest Sunday of all time.

On the day following the crucifixion the disciples kept silence. They found a place of quietness and of fellowship in the upper room of the goodman of the house. The Passover sacrifices were being offered in the temple, and its courts were thronged by people. But the disciples knew that they dared not enter into the streets, and they had no desire to share in the sacrifices of the priests who had plotted to crucify their Master.

But there was one loving heart which knew neither fear nor shame. Mary Magdalene adored Jesus in an unquestioning faith. She had been a poor, tormented, shrieking girl, possessed by seven devils. Jesus, in His compassion, had cast them out, and she had sat at His feet to listen to Him in her right mind. So after this quiet day was over, Mary Magdalene rose early in the morning, when it was yet dark, and, along with some other women, she went out to visit the tomb in which Jesus had been laid.

As these women stole silently out of the city, they remembered that the grave, which had been hewn out of the rock, was closed by a great stone placed against its mouth. They were wondering who would roll away this stone, for they wished to see the face of Jesus again, and to pour fresh spices on His body. To their surprise, the stone had been taken away. Mary stooped down and looked in, and she saw that the grave was empty. She sped back to the city, and found Peter and John, and she cried, with sobs and tears, " They have taken away the Lord out of the sepulchre, and we know not where they have laid Him."

Peter and John hastened out to the garden to see if Mary's story was true. John was the younger man, and he ran more swiftly, and came first to the grave. He looked in and saw that the body of Jesus was not there, but he did not go inside. When Peter came to the tomb, he went in, and he saw the linen clothes, in which the body of Jesus had been wrapped, lying folded, and the napkin, which had been tied round His head, in a place by itself. They saw that when Jesus had left the tomb, He did so without haste, and left His grave clothes in good order behind Him.

Peter and John, and the women who had come out with Mary Magdalene, went back to Jerusalem, greatly wondering. A new hope had been kindled in their hearts, but they were still doubtful and sorrowful. But Mary stayed beside the grave weeping. She stooped down and looked in, and saw two angels in white sitting, one at the head, and the other at the feet, where the body of Jesus had been lying. The angels asked her, "Woman, why weepest thou?" She said, "Because they have taken away my Lord, and I know not where they have laid Him." As she turned away in deep grief, she saw Jesus standing on the path to the grave. She did not know that it was Jesus, for He was so greatly changed. He was no longer weary, and His face was not clouded by sorrow. It was bright with the shining of His joy in having overcome sin and death. She thought this stranger must be the gardener, and so she said to him, "Sir, if thou have borne Him hence, tell me where thou hast laid Him, and I will take Him away."

Jesus said to her, very tenderly, "Mary!" She

knew His voice at once. She had heard it first when He healed her of her madness by speaking His word of power. She had often listened to it as He taught. She gave him one look of wonderful reverence, and then she bowed down before Him and said, " My Master ! " She drew nearer to Him, but Jesus had to tell her that He had no longer a body which could be touched, and no longer wore the garments of men. So He said to her, " Touch Me not, for I am not yet ascended to My Father : but go to My brethren, and say unto them, I ascend unto My Father, and your Father ; and to My God and your God." Mary Magdalene left the garden, and went back to Jerusalem, and told the disciples that she had seen the Lord, and that He had spoken these things to her.

When Mary told the disciples all her story they were amazed. The deep darkness which had shadowed their minds had passed away. They began to recall to each other what Jesus had said about being put to death, and about rising again from the dead. They still wondered whether it was really true that Jesus was alive, and they began to hope that they would see His face, and hear Him speak as Mary had done. For some of them thought that Mary had only seen some one like Jesus, and they still doubted. But, before the close of the day, Jesus was seen of nearly all His disciples, and in the evening they were filled with a great wonder, and a new joy in their Master, who had shown His power, even over death.

We call this great day when Jesus arose from the

dead by the name of Easter Sunday. Every year as it comes round, all who believe in Jesus remember that He came out of the tomb, and made Himself known to His disciples, and spoke to them of His love and grace. It was the gladdest Sunday to the disciples, and it will be so to all who know Jesus and believe in Him, to the end of time, and in heaven for ever.

THE EVENING OF EASTER DAY

The wonder and the joy of the glad Easter Sunday had not come to its full, when Mary Magdalene told the disciples that Jesus had risen from the dead. Jesus knew that they found it hard to believe, and so He showed Himself alive to many others, and He spoke to them, with His own love and power, until their doubt passed away.

That same afternoon, two of His disciples set out to walk to Emmaus, a village about seven miles from Jerusalem. The name of one of these disciples was Cleopas, but we do not know the name of the other. They were not apostles, but merely simple members of the company of believers. As they walked they began to talk together about Jesus, and His wondrous works, and His power and grace as a prophet. They grew dejected as they recalled His cruel death, and began to feel how great was their loss.

A stranger joined them, and he asked them, " What manner of communications are these that ye have one to another, as ye walk and are sad ? " They looked at this stranger, but they did not know him to be Jesus. They told him that they had been speaking about Jesus of Nazareth, and of their grief that the chief priests and the Roman Governor had condemned Him to death, and had crucified Him. They wondered that he did not know of these happenings, and they said to him, that he must be merely a visitor, who had come to the Passover from some far country. Then they said that their deepest sorrow was that they had hoped that Jesus, who was now dead and buried, would have redeemed Israel from their bondage to the Roman power.

Then they told him the strangest part of the story, that some of their women friends had gone out to the grave of Jesus early that morning, and had seen a vision of angels, who had told them that Jesus was alive. They added that some of the disciples had gone out to the tomb, and had found it empty, but they had not seen Jesus.

Jesus listened to their words, and then He said, " Oh, foolish ones, and slow of heart to believe all that the prophets have spoken ; ought not Christ to have suffered these things, and to enter into His glory ? " All the rest of the way He spoke to them about Himself, and explained what all the prophets had foretold, and how clearly it had all been fulfilled.

The two men listened with kindling hearts, so that, when they came to their house in the village they asked Him to come in with them, but He made as though He would go farther on. But they pressed Him, and said, "Abide with us; for it is toward evening, and the day is far spent." He went in with them, and He sat down at their table. Then He took bread, and, following the old custom, He gave thanks, and He broke the bread, and gave it to them. They had seen Jesus do that before, and, in a moment, their eyes were opened, and they knew Him. When Jesus saw that they knew who He was, He vanished out of their sight.

The two men were greatly amazed, and they rose up at once, and hastened back to Jerusalem, and burst in upon the disciples who were gathered together in the upper room, for the evening had now come. They found that the doors of the room were shut, for the disciples were still in fear of the hate of the priests and scribes. When they entered into the room they told the disciples that Jesus had come to them on the way to Emmaus, and had spoken to them, but that they had not known Him until He had broken the bread. While the apostles were listening with beating hearts to their story, a hush fell upon the room, and Jesus Himself stood there in the midst of them, and said to them, " Peace be unto you." At first they were terrified, and they trembled, and supposed that they had seen a spirit. But Jesus showed them His hands and His feet, with the print of the nails driven in when He was hung upon the cross. Their doubt was gone, and a great gladness filled their hearts, and Jesus lifted up His hands and said, " Peace be unto you; as My Father hath sent Me, even so send I you. Receive ye the Holy Ghost."

Now one of the apostles, named Thomas, was not with them that night, when Jesus came to the upper room. When the disciples saw him, they said, with exultant joy, " We have seen the Lord." But Thomas said, " Except I shall see in His hands the print of the nails, and put my finger into the print of the nails, and thrust my hand into His side, I will not believe."

The next Sunday evening the disciples assembled in the same place, and the doors again were shut. This time Thomas was with them. Again Jesus came and said to them, " Peace be unto you." Then He turned to Thomas, who was looking on, in awe-struck silence, and said to him, " Reach hither thy finger, and behold My hands ; and reach hither thy hand, and thrust it into My side ; and be not faithless but believing." As He heard the voice of Jesus, and as he saw how deeply Jesus loved him, and re-membered how often He had spoken in the same kind and eager way, Thomas saw that this was indeed Jesus, who had risen from the dead. He bowed down before Him, and said, " My Lord, and my God." Then Jesus said to him, that all those who would hereafter believe in Him would be blessed indeed.

It was in this way that Jesus showed Himself to the men and women, who had known Him when He kept company with them, as He went about doing good. And as they beheld Him, and heard Him speak, they became confident, and certain, that He was the Son of God, and that God had raised Him from the dead.

The Morning on the Shore

We are told that when Jesus appeared to Mary Magdalene in the garden, He bade her go to the disciples with the message that they should go into Galilee, and there He would meet them. He knew that they were living in fear of the Jews, and that if they went about declaring that they had seen Him, and that He was alive, and had risen from the dead, the chief priests and scribes would lay hold upon them, and punish them.

So the disciples left Jerusalem, and went back to Capernaum, and waited for the day when Jesus would again stand in their midst, and say, " Peace be unto you," and they would again behold the print of the nails in His hands and in His feet. One day seven of them were together. These seven were Peter, and Thomas, and Nathanael, with Peter and John, and two other disciples. They were waiting for the coming of Jesus, and had begun to grow weary and restless. So Peter said, " I am going to fish," and the others at once joined him and said, " We also will go with thee." They went down to the shore, and prepared their net, and launched their boat, and sailed out to the deeper water.

That night they caught nothing. When the morning was come they made for the shore, tired and disappointed. When they came near they saw a stranger standing not far from the place where they meant to land. They did not recognise the stranger, or think that he was Jesus. They heard him call to them, and ask, as the fish merchants of Capernaum used to do, " Lads, have ye any fish ? " When they cried back " No," he said to them, " Cast the net

Galilean Boats.

on the right side of the boat, and ye shall find." They thought that this stranger had seen fish leaping up and rippling the water, so they cast their net, and now they found it so full that they could not draw it on board of their boat.

They looked at this stranger on the shore in surprise, and John, whom Jesus loved so much, kept his eyes fixed upon him. The tones of his voice were familiar.

His knowledge of the place where fish could be found was so strange, and, above all, his compassion on weary men who had toiled all night and caught nothing, was so like Jesus, that it flashed into his mind that this was their Master. So he said to Peter, " It is the Lord." Peter had only to hear his words to recognise Jesus, and, in his quick and eager way, he put on his fisher's coat, plunged into the sea, and swam to the shore. The other disciples got into their smallboat, and pulled to the shore, towing the net, full of fishes, behind them.

They all gathered around Jesus, just as in the old days, delighted at seeing His face again. They noticed that a fire had been kindled, and a few fish were broiled upon it, and a loaf of bread was lying at hand. They were hungry after the long night, and they remembered how often Jesus had showed compassion on the hungry. Jesus bade them bring some of the fish which they had caught. Peter went to the net and found that, although there had been a great catch, and the net was quite full, it had not been broken. He counted the fish, and there were one hundred and fifty-three. When he had brought back a few, and they were made ready, Jesus said, " Come and have breakfast." They sat down, and Jesus with His own hands served them with bread and fish.

Now Peter had been looking at Jesus with a troubled mind and with questioning eyes. He could not forget that night, when he had boasted that he would never deny Jesus, and he was sitting ashamed and miserable as he remembered that he had forsaken Him and fled, and had said, with oaths and curses, " I know not the Man." He had repented, with a true sorrow and a deep shame, and he had been forgiven. But he was afraid that Jesus would never be quite the same to him as He had been.

Jesus knew Peter's thoughts, and He saw that Peter did not know how fully he had been forgiven, and how greatly Jesus intended to honour him, and, as He looked at him, He began to speak to him, so as to restore his peace and his joy.

He said to him, " Simon, son of Jonas, lovest thou Me more than these." Peter replied, " Yea, Lord ; Thou knowest that I love Thee." Then Jesus said, " Feed My lambs." A second time He asked him, " Simon, son of Jonas, lovest thou Me ? " Peter replied, " Yea, Lord ; Thou knowest that I love Thee," and Jesus said, " Feed My sheep."

A third time He asked him the same question. Peter was grieved because He had asked this question three times, for it seemed to show that Jesus was not sure that Peter loved Him. So he cried very humbly, " Lord, Thou knowest all things ; Thou knowest that I love Thee." Then Jesus said, and He spoke with tender feeling, " Feed My sheep." In this way, Jesus made it clear to Peter himself, and to all the disciples, how much He desired the love of Peter, and how high and holy was the service to which He had called him. Then He told him that when he would grow old, he would suffer nobly and bravely for Christ's sake, and at last he would die for his Lord and Master. Peter listened, with a heart throbbing with a new hope, and his love to Christ was like a deep well whose waters never failed. Jesus saw and rejoiced in Peter's faith, and He added, as a counsel he should never forget, " Follow Me."

While Jesus was speaking to Peter another disciple had been coming toward them. This disciple was John. He was the youngest of the band, and so deeply beloved by Jesus that he was called " the disciple whom Jesus loved." He always sat next to Jesus at the table. When Peter heard the footstep behind him he turned quickly round and he saw John. At once he asked Jesus, " Lord, and what shall this man do ? " He was wondering what would happen to John in those sad days to come, when he would suffer death for Christ. But Jesus does not wish us to be curious about other people, or to ask questions about what God desires them to do. So He said to Peter, " If I will that he tarry till I come, what is that to thee ? Follow thou Me."

Some of the disciples who heard this saying thought that it meant that John would not die until Jesus came again. But Jesus meant that John would not end his life as Peter would. And we know that John lived long after all the other disciples died, and that he was greatly beloved by all Christian people. His white hair and his shining face were the marks of his holiness. When he grew very old, he was carried into the Church, and the people sat, hushed and still, as he lifted his hand and said, " Little children, love one another." He told again the story of the life of Jesus, and no part of it he loved to tell with more delight than this story of the morning on the shore.

CHRIST'S FAREWELL

For forty days Jesus had showed Himself alive, as the risen Lord, to His disciples. In the garden of Joseph of Arimathæa, by the highway to Emmaus, in the upper room at Jerusalem, on the shore of the Sea of Galilee, and in other places whose names have not been told us, Jesus appeared in His glory, and they all knew Him to be Christ, the Son of God. They saw Him to be the same Jesus who had told them that He had come from His Father in heaven to teach them God's love, and to die on the cross for their sins. When the forty days were coming to their close, He appointed a special meeting with them to bid them farewell.

He bade them return to Jerusalem, and to wait there until He came. He knew that they were somewhat afraid of the rulers, but He gave them His command that they should be of good courage, and should not depart from the city. The place of meeting was to be the upper room, where they had so often gathered, for it was a room very dear, both to Himself and His disciples.

When they were gathered together, Jesus gave them a great promise. He knew He was going to leave them, but He wished to bestow one last blessing upon them. That blessing was the gift of the Holy Ghost, and He told them that they must wait until the blessing came. So He said to them, " Wait for the promise of the Father, which ye have heard of Me. For John truly baptized with water, but ye shall be baptized with the Holy Ghost, not many days hence." By that promise, Jesus meant to tell them that God would give them His spirit, to dwell in their hearts, and to make them pure and true, and to enable them to be strong and brave and loving in their service to Him.

The disciples heard this great promise, but they did not understand it. Even while Jesus spoke, they were still craving for the earthly kingdom with its worldly power, as all the Jewish people desired. They knew Him to have such wonderful power, and were sure He was the promised Christ, and now they thought He would use His power, to make Himself a King. So they asked Him, " Lord, wilt Thou, at this time, restore again the Kingdom of Israel ? " Jesus must have been somewhat grieved that these disciples were still asking for an earthly kingdom. Yet He only said, very gently, " It is not for you to know the times or the seasons, which the Father hath put in His own power." Then He said again that they would receive God's Spirit, and they would bear witness to Him throughout the whole world.

They left the upper room, and passed through the streets of the city, and went out to walk along the

old dearly-loved road that led up the slope of the
Mount of Olives, to Bethany. It was near the season
which we now know as Whitsuntide—the loveliest
time of the year in all lands. It was a beautiful
summer day. The valleys were covered with ripening
corn. Every hillside was gay with flowers. A great
joy was shining in Christ's face, and a deep peace
filled the disciples' hearts. When they came near
to Bethany Jesus stood still, and a hush fell upon the
little company. There Jesus bade them farewell.
As He spoke He ascended from among them into the
heavens. They looked up in speechless wonder,
until a cloud received Him out of their sight.

While they were looking up into the heavens to see
if He might not return again, two men stood beside
them in white garments, and asked, " Ye men of
Galilee, why stand ye gazing up into heaven ? this
same Jesus which is taken up from you into heaven,
shall so come in like manner as ye have seen Him
go into heaven." So the disciples retraced their
steps, and came back to Jerusalem. They went into
the upper room, and gathered around about them
the believers in Jesus, both men and women, who
had known Him when He taught the people, and had
seen Him when He rose from the dead. Day after
day, for ten days, they met to continue in prayer,
and to strengthen their faith in the Lord Jesus.

There was a feast of the Jews which was called the
feast of Pentecost, because it was held fifty days after
the Passover. On the morning of that day, the

disciples were gathered together in the upper room. As they were praying, there came a sound as of a mighty rushing wind out of the heavens. This wind passed over Jerusalem, and in a strong current swept into the upper room, and there appeared spurts of fire over the heads of the disciples. They were all deeply moved, and their hearts were filled with a new sense of God, and His nearness, and His love, so that they had a new courage and a new power. That was the coming of the Holy Ghost.

They went out to speak to the people, for the city was full of strangers. Those who heard them were astonished, and those who had known them before simply as Galilean fishermen, and followers of that Jesus of Nazareth who had been crucified, said to each other, "What meaneth this?". Then Peter rose and told them that this was the power of God's spirit, and he said, "Ye men of Israel, hear these words; Jesus of Nazareth, whom ye have taken, and by wicked hands have crucified and slain, God hath raised up. Therefore let all the house of Israel know assuredly, that God hath made that same Jesus, whom ye crucified, both Lord and Christ." That was the message first proclaimed by Peter and the other disciples, and is now being declared to the uttermost parts of the earth. It is the message of the Risen Saviour.

Now that is the message that all who love Christ rejoice to hear. The great hymns, both for grown-up people and little children, which are sung with

glad voices and shining faces, tell us again and again
" The Lord has risen." But the people who heard
this message, when it was first spoken by Peter, did
not rejoice. They were cast into fear and shame.
They were pricked in their heart, for they saw how
cruel had been their deed, and how wicked had been
their thoughts when they crucified Jesus. So they cried
out, " Men and brethren, what shall we do ? " Then
Peter went on to tell them that Jesus loved even those
who put Him to death, and that God forgave all who
were truly sorry for their sin. So whenever any one
comes to Jesus vexed and ashamed, and confesses
his wrong-doing, God is full of forgiveness, and He
completes His mercy by giving them His Holy Spirit.

Every Whitsuntide good people who love Jesus
Christ recall these great days. On one Sunday they
rejoice in His ascension into heaven. Then on another
they remember this coming of the Spirit of God to
make the people of God glad and brave. In days
gone by they used to dress in white garments to show
their joy. We may not do this in our lands, for we
have less sunshine than they had. But we should
have as deep a joy in our hearts.

THE FIRST WITNESSES TO THE FAITH

At the Temple Gate

EVERY one who saw the disciples in those great days after Jesus ascended to heaven, wondered at the change they saw in them. They were filled with a new courage and power and joy. They no longer feared the priests, who wondered at their boldness. When they gathered together, or met each other in the street, their faces shone, as they said to each other, "Christ is risen." But strangest of all was their new wisdom and power. They were simple and unlearned men, yet when they spoke, the people listened with deep attention, and they went among the people doing wonders and miracles of compassion.

The first of these miracles was wrought at one of the gates of the temple. It was called the Beautiful Gate, because of the lovely lily-work carved upon its pillars, and the rich scrolls upon its doors. Jesus had always gone to the temple at the Jewish hours of prayer, and He had taken His disciples along with Him. They continued this custom, and so Peter and John, who had become dear friends and close companions, went up to the temple every day, to pray in its court.

One day, about three o'clock in the afternoon,

when they were about to pass in, they saw a lame man, lying on his mat, beside the gate. He was a very poor man, and his friends carried him there every day, that he might sit and beg. Peter remembered that Jesus had always shown compassion to the lame. He believed that God had given him the spirit of Jesus, and that he could heal this poor lame man, in Christ's name. So when he heard the poor man's plaint, he stopped and looked upon him, and John stopped along with him.

Then Peter fastened his eyes upon him with a very intent look, and said to him, " Look on us." The lame man looked up to Peter's face, and held out his hand, expecting to receive a gift. But Peter did not mean to give him money, for he also was poor. So he said, " Silver and gold have I none ; but such as I have give I thee : in the name of Jesus Christ of Nazareth, rise up and walk." The man had heard of Jesus of Nazareth, and of His miracles of healing the lame. He saw how entirely Peter trusted in the power of Jesus to heal him. So when Peter took hold of his outstretched hand with his firm grasp, a new faith filled his heart, and a thrill of recovered strength passed through him. His shrunken ankles received power, and his withered and helpless feet became strong, and he leaped up, and began to walk, as he had not done for many years. He passed into the temple along with Peter and John, walking and leaping in the gladness of his new strength, and praising God aloud until all the people in the temple court heard him.

His cries of grateful delight soon gathered a crowd around him and Peter and John. When the people saw him they knew him well, for he was about forty years of age, and they had often passed him as he sat and begged for alms at the temple gate. They looked in wonder and amazement at what had happened to him. The lame man was so filled with gratitude, that he would not let Peter and John go, but clung to them as a little child might keep close to his father and mother. So when the crowd began to press upon them, Peter led the people into a side court, called " Solomon's Porch." It had been built by King Solomon, and it was a quiet corridor, where men could walk when the temple court was full. Jesus used to teach in this porch, and Peter, remembering his Master's custom, led the people that he might speak to them there. When they were gathered round him, and quietness had fallen upon the company, Peter stood up to tell them of Jesus and of His power.

He began by asking the people not to look on himself and on John as having any power to work miracles. He saw that the people were looking at them with reverence, and would pay them too much honour. So he said, " Ye men of Israel, why marvel ye at this ? or why look ye so earnestly on us, as though, by our own power or holiness, we had made this man to walk?" Then he told them, in words of sorrow and reproach, all that the chief priests and Pilate had done to Jesus when they released Barabbas, as the people had desired, and hung Jesus on the cross. Then he came to what he was eager to declare. He told them that God had raised Jesus from the dead, and he declared, " His name, through faith in His name, hath made this man strong whom ye see and know." Then he spoke more gently, telling them that it was through ignorance that this was done, and he called upon them to repent that they might be forgiven. As the people listened to Peter, they were moved, and about five thousand became believers in Jesus and followers of Him.

As the day was drawing to a close, the priests and the rulers of the temple came upon them. Some one had gone to them, and told them what had happened, and what Peter had been saying. They were annoyed that Peter had taught the people that Jesus, whom they crucified, had risen from the dead. So they took Peter and John, and, as it was about six o'clock, they put them into the prison for the night. In the morning they were brought before the priests and scribes and were questioned. But Peter and John quite calmly declared their faith in Jesus Christ. The rulers and priests could not make any charge against them, so they let them go, with a strict warning that they must not speak or teach in the name of Jesus. Peter and John answered, " Whether it be right in the sight of God to hearken unto you more than unto God, judge ye. For we cannot but speak the things which we have seen and heard."

The Martyrdom of Stephen

Before Jesus ascended to heaven He told His disciples that they must be witnesses to Him to the uttermost parts of the earth. By bearing witness He did not mean simply telling the people of His love and power. He meant that they must live pure and brave lives, as He did, and suffer, and even die, for Him. They did not forget His words, for some of them were stoned, some were slain by the sword, some were crucified, and some were thrown to the lions. The first of these witnesses to die for Christ was a young man named Stephen.

Many of the people who had become followers of Jesus were very poor. Some of them were widows who were often almost starving. So the kind-hearted apostles, who remembered how Jesus fed the hungry, provided a daily meal for these poor women. But the apostles were busy all day long in preaching and teaching, and when they began to provide a daily portion for the widows, they were overburdened, and some of the poor women thought themselves neglected. So the apostles asked the people to choose seven men who would serve the tables at the daily meal, and Stephen was the first of the seven who were chosen.

Now Stephen was an able and well-trained young man. He had been taught the Scriptures from his boyhood, and he knew many of their great passages by heart. He had rejoiced in proving from the

Scriptures that Jesus was the promised Messiah.
He was a clear and eloquent speaker, so that when he
addressed the Jews in the synagogues, they could
not withstand the spirit and power of his speech.
So he became known as a young believer, who was
doing great wonders and miracles among the people.

When the same priests and scribes who had crucified

St. Stephen's Gate.

Jesus heard of Stephen and of his power with the
people, they took him and brought him before their
council. They gave money to false witnesses to
declare that he had spoken against Moses and against
God, and had said that Jesus would destroy the
temple, and change all their customs. It was the
same charge as they had made against Jesus, when

He stood in the same place before the high priest. Stephen remembered that Jesus had been accused, and he was throbbing with a deep joy that he should suffer as Jesus did. That joy was seen when " all that sat in the council, looking steadfastly on him, saw his face as it had been the face of an angel."

Stephen made no answer to these charges. But the high priest did not wish to condemn Stephen without hearing what he had to say, so he asked him, "Are these things so ? " Then Stephen began at the very beginning of the history of God's dealing with the people of Israel. He reminded them how dearly God had loved them and how He had cared for them.

Then he passed on to show that He had sent them many prophets and righteous men. But he grew bolder and spoke with deeper feeling when he declared that the Jewish people had not listened to these prophets and had often refused to hear them, and had scorned and rejected them. Then he closed by saying, "As your fathers did, so do ye. Which of the prophets have not your fathers persecuted ? and they have slain them which showed before of the coming of the Just One ; of whom ye have been now the betrayers and murderers."

They had listened in silence to Stephen's fervent speech. But at his severe rebuke, they were cut to the heart, and they rose up with loud cries and gnashed upon him with their teeth. Stephen knew no fear, for he looked up to heaven, and he said, " Behold I see the heavens opened, and the Son of Man standing on the right hand of God."

Stephen's heavenly calm in the council had amazed them. His thrilling address kept them silent. His closing charge provoked them to anger. But when he declared that he saw Jesus, at God's right hand, they were roused to madness. In their fury they uttered fierce shouts, and they put their fingers into their ears, and then the whole company rushed at Stephen, and carried him through the streets of the city, and outside of the gate, to stone him.

Now one of the most merciless members of this council was a young man named Saul. He had heard Stephen speak in the synagogue, and Stephen's power and boldness roused his intense anger. He loved his nation with a keen devotion. He believed that the Jews were God's people, and that no other race could be so dear to God. He thought that the Law and the Temple were so holy, that no one should be allowed to say one word against them. He had always hated and opposed those who had spoken in the name of Jesus. Now, as he sat to listen to Stephen, his anger blazed out. He became foremost in laying hold on Stephen and in leading him out of the city. He stood to see him die, and the witnesses, who always cast the first stone at those they accused, laid their outer garments at Saul's feet.

Stephen's death was followed by many consequences. The Christian people made great lamentation over him. They took up his poor mangled body, and gave it burial, and went back to their homes heavy with grief. The chief priests and scribes resolved to take sterner measures against the followers of Jesus, and young Saul of Tarsus became the foremost among the persecutors. But what he saw and heard that day when Stephen died, he never forgot. He saw him standing meekly when the stones began to crash upon him. He saw him when he fell upon his knees and prayed, " Lord Jesus, receive my spirit." He heard him, before he died, praying that strange prayer, in a loud, clear voice, " Lord, lay not this sin to their charge." He left the scene with a deeper hate, but with a conscience which would some day condemn him.

On the Way to Damascus

Saul, the young, hot-hearted Pharisee, who took the foremost part in the stoning of Stephen, belonged to Tarsus, a town of Asia Minor. His father and mother were Jews who had left their native land, but were most devout in their faith. They had brought up young Saul in all the strict customs of Jewish worship. He had been educated in a Jewish school at Tarsus, and had been taught the Old Testament scriptures from his childhood. When he was about seventeen years of age he was sent to Jerusalem to be a student under its famous teachers. He had been a clever boy at school, and soon became known as a young man of clear knowledge and great powers of argument and of speech. He was so loyal to the Jewish faith that he thought he was pleasing God in scorning the name of Jesus, and in persecuting his followers to the death.

The priests and the rulers had been becoming more and more alarmed at the increasing number of those who were naming Jesus Christ as Lord. The boldness and the power of Stephen were so great that they began to take extreme measures against the Christian people, and they cast all of them, on whom they could lay hands, into prison. The persecuted believers fled out of Jerusalem into the country round about, and some of them travelled as far away as Damascus. Yet they were so true to Jesus that, as they went everywhere, when they were scattered abroad, they told the story of Jesus and His love, and they proclaimed His resurrection from the dead, so that great numbers of the people believed in Him.

This aroused young Saul to an intense zeal. He broke forth into angry threats, and he asked the High Priest to give him letters to the synagogues in Damascus, so that he might lay hold on any who named Christ's name and bring them back to Jerusalem, to stand their trial before the council as Stephen had done.

Now Saul, whom we know better by the name of Paul, was quite sincere. But he did not know the truth about Jesus, and he did not dream that Jesus loved him, and longed after him as a disciple. As the company, with which he travelled, came to the high ridge above Damascus, and looked down upon that beautiful old city, about the midday hour, a great light suddenly shone round about them. Paul was dazzled and blinded, and he fell to the ground. As he lay in helplessness, he heard a voice saying to him, " Saul, Saul, why persecutest thou Me ? " He asked in surprise, " Who art Thou, Lord ? " The answer came, " I am Jesus, whom thou persecutest ? it is hard for thee to kick against the pricks."

Now this appeal of Jesus went home to Paul's inmost heart. He had been quite sure that Jesus was not the Son of God. But as he had listened to Stephen, and had marked the triumph of his death, and as he recalled all that the prophets had said of Jesus, he began to be troubled in mind, although he would not confess how vexed he was at himself. He tried to stifle the feelings which were arising in his heart. But when Jesus said that he was like the dull-minded oxen who kicked against the iron-pointed goads of their drivers, and only hurt themselves, he saw that some one, who knew his heart and mind, was speaking to him. In the moment he was assured that Jesus was alive, and had risen from the dead. He trembled in his astonishment, and said very humbly, " Lord, what wilt Thou have me to do ? " Then Jesus answered him, "Arise, and go into the city, and it shall be told thee what thou must do."

The other members of Paul's party had seen the bright light, and they had heard the voice, but they saw no one. When Paul arose from the earth, he opened his eyes, but he found that he was blind, so he was led by his companions into Damascus and sat alone, in the darkness, for three days, neither eating nor drinking, sorrowing in his heart that he had so persecuted Christ and His disciples.

The leader of the Christian people in Damascus was a disciple named Ananias. God called him in a vision and said to him, "Arise, and go into the street which is called Straight, and inquire in the house of Judas for one called Saul of Tarsus, for, behold, he prayeth." Ananias wondered if this could be God's command, and he answered, " Lord, I have heard by many of this man, how much evil he hath done to Thy saints at Jerusalem ! and here, he hath authority from the chief priests to bind all that call on Thy name." But the Lord said to him, " Go thy way : for he is a chosen vessel unto Me, to bear My name before the Gentiles, and kings, and the children of Israel."

Ananias at once went to the street called Straight, and found the house where Paul was living, and went in and took him by both hands, with the kindly words, " Brother Saul, the Lord, even Jesus, that appeared unto thee in the way that thou camest, hath sent me, that thou mightest receive thy sight, and be filled with the Holy Ghost." Immediately Paul's sight was restored. He arose and was baptized and took his place in the little company of the believers. He sat down with them, and prayed their prayers, and sang their hymns of praise to Christ. Then he went into the Jewish synagogue, and by his clear knowledge of the Scriptures and his power of speech he proved that Jesus was the Son of God.

Every one was amazed to see that Saul, the persecutor, had become Paul, the loyal follower of Jesus Christ. But the Jews began to hate him with an anger fiercer than had burned in their hatred of any other believer. They began to lie in wait to seize him, and they watched at the gates to take him if he should try to escape. But one of the Christian people had a house which was built on the wall of the city, and Paul was taken there, and let down outside the wall from a window in a basket, and, after a time, he returned to Jerusalem to preach Christ.

DORCAS

After a while the bitter and revengeful persecution of the Christian people ceased. The priests and the rulers saw that the followers of Jesus did not yield, but rather grew bolder, when they were being hunted and cast into prison. They loved Jesus more deeply because they suffered for Him. So the little assemblies of Christian people, who were gathered together to worship Christ enjoyed a time of peace, and large numbers of the people were added to the Church of Christ.

But these early Christians were often simple people, and they were eager for instruction in the gospel of

their Lord. They had an especial desire to see and
to hear some of the apostles, who had companied
with Jesus, when He went about doing good, and had
seen Him after He arose from the dead. So Peter
left Jerusalem to go through the land, visiting these
little congregations, to tell them what Jesus had said
and what He had done, and to strengthen their faith

The Traditional House of Simon the Tanner.

in Him. As he went he received the spirit of Jesus,
and he not only spake with power, but he did miracles
in the name of Jesus.

He came in his journeyings to a little town named
Lydda, that lies in the plain, not far from the sea.
He went into the meeting of the Christian people,
and he preached to them. After the service was
over, they told him of one of their number whose

name was Æneas. He was a believer in Jesus, but he could not come to the place of prayer, because he was afflicted with palsy. This dreadful disease, in which a constant trembling afflicts the whole body, so that the hands and the feet shake continually, was thought to be incurable. Æneas had lain in bed for eight years, and his fellow-believers looked at him with a constant pity.

Peter went at once to his house. As he went, he remembered a man who had been sick of the palsy, and had lain helpless and friendless, by the pool of Bethesda. He remembered the words that Jesus had spoken to him, " Take up thy bed and walk." He knew that Jesus would have spoken the same words, had He stood in the house of Æneas. So he went in and said to him, "Æneas, Jesus Christ maketh thee whole ; arise and make thy bed." Æneas arose from his bed to find that his trembling and shaking had gone, and all the people of the district turned to the Lord.

A few miles farther on, right upon the sea coast there was a town, called Joppa. It is still a well-known seaport, now known by the name of Jaffa. There was, in the little Christian church in Joppa, a woman named Tabitha, or, as we know her better, Dorcas. She was a woman of wealth, with a large house of many rooms. She might have lived an easy, self-pleasing life, and spent her money on rich living and costly clothing. But she was a true follower of Jesus, and she filled all her days with good works.

She visited the sick and gave of her means to the needy. She took an especial care of the poor widows and their children, and took great pains to clothe them when they were so poor as not to be able to buy garments for themselves. She was one of the first women to understand that Jesus had called women to a service of kindness to all who are in need.

Now all the people loved her, and her very name was dear to them. So when she fell sick and died, they were all stricken with sorrow. She died while Peter was at Lydda, and when the Christians in Joppa heard of the healing of Æneas, they resolved to send to Lydda, and ask Peter to come to them. With a heavy heart they prepared her body for burial, for in the warm climates of the East, people who die are buried on the same day. So they laid her, prepared for the grave, in one of her upper rooms. Yet some of them cherished the hope that Peter might come to them in their sorrow.

So two of the members of the little church were sent to Lydda to ask Peter to come without delay. Peter remembered not only that Jesus Himself arose from the dead, but that He had recalled the little daughter of Jairus, and had raised the son of the widow of Nain, as he was being carried to his burial, and that He had called forth Lazarus out of the grave, after he had been four days dead. It was only nine miles from Lydda to Joppa, and Peter at once went back with the two men who had been sent to him.

When Peter reached the house of Dorcas they took

him to the upper room where the body was lying. There he found the women wailing and lamenting, and, along with them, the poor widows who showed him the garments she had made for them. Peter remembered that when Jesus had come to the house of Jairus and had heard the shrill wailing and loud lamenting of the mourners, He asked them to leave the room, and to hush their cries. So now he put all the mourners out, and stillness prevailed. He did not think that he had any power to raise the dead. He knew that God alone, who gave life once, could give it again. So he kneeled down by the dead body and he prayed. Then he arose and looked upon Dorcas, and said, " Tabitha, arise." Dorcas opened her eyes, and looked at him. She had never seen him before, and she was amazed. But she sat up, and he gave her his hand to help her to arise. Then he called the company, who had been mourning for her, and presented Dorcas to them alive and well.

The Christian people in Joppa were so gladdened, that they went about telling every one of this wonderful arising from the dead. Many joined their company, and they begged Peter to stay with them for a while. One of their members, Simon, a tanner, received Peter into his house, and every day Peter preached Jesus as God's Son who had risen from the dead.

THE ROMAN SOLDIER

Cornelius was the centurion, or captain, of a band of Roman soldiers stationed at Cæsarea, about thirty miles northward from Joppa. He was a good man, of a devout mind, and he no longer worshipped heathen gods, but feared the Lord with all his household. He offered daily prayer at the hours observed by the Jews, and he gave large gifts to the poor.

Cornelius had first heard of Jesus when Pilate put Him to death on the cross. When the persecuted Christian people fled from Jerusalem, some of them came to Cæsarea, and he heard the strange story that Jesus had risen from the dead. Then the report that Peter had restored Dorcas to life was brought to him, and he began to wonder, with a deep interest, about Jesus.

One afternoon, about three o'clock, he was praying in secret at the usual hour. An angel from God came in to him, and named him, "Cornelius." He was afraid, when he saw the shining angel, and he asked, "What is it, Lord?" He was answered, "Thy prayers and thine alms are come up for a memorial before God." The angel told him to send men to Joppa, and to ask Peter, who would tell him what he ought to do.

Cornelius at once called two of his servants, and a soldier, who also feared God, to guard them by the way. He told them of his vision, and he sent them to

Joppa with a request that Peter should come to him. As they were approaching Joppa on the following day, about twelve o'clock, Peter was praying in the quietness of the flat roof of the house of Simon the tanner. He had been fasting from food, and was hungry and faint. He fell into a trance and he dreamed. In his dream he saw a great white sheet, held by the four corners, let down from heaven. It was full of all manner of beasts, and of birds, and of creeping things. Then he heard a voice saying to him, " Rise, Peter, kill and eat." But the Jews would not eat such beasts and creeping creatures as he saw in the sheet. So Peter answered, " Not so, Lord ; for I have never eaten anything that is common or unclean." The voice replied, " What God hath cleansed, that call not thou common or unclean."

Peter could not think what this vision might mean. Up to this time all the disciples of Jesus had been Jews, and they thought that neither Greeks nor Romans, nor any of the heathen nations, should worship with them, or even sit down at the same table. As he was doubting what the vision meant, the three men from Cornelius, who had been inquiring for him, were standing at the gate. While he was still wondering about his vision, God whispered to him that he was to go down, and to hear their request, and to accompany them without doubt in his heart.

When Peter met the three men they told him their errand. Then Peter began to see some meaning in the message of the angel. Cornelius was a Gentile, and was unclean to a Jew. But the angel had said, "What God hath cleansed, call not thou common." So when he heard that they came from Cornelius he called them in, and he gave them lodging for the night. In the morning, accompanied by some of the Christian men of Joppa, he set out with them to go to Cornelius.

When Peter came to Cæsarea, Cornelius received him with great courtesy. He had gathered a number of his kinsmen and other friends to meet him. So when Peter went into the centurion's room he found them waiting to listen to him. When Peter stood up to speak to them, he saw that they were all Gentiles, and, in a flash, he knew, beyond all doubt, what God had meant to teach him in his heavenly vision. He was aware what some of these Gentiles who had come to the house of Cornelius would think of one, who was born a Jew, keeping their company. So at once he said, " Ye know how that it is an unlawful thing for a man that is a Jew to keep company, or come unto one of another nation ; but God hath showed me that I should not call any man common or unclean." It was a strange and a beautiful thing for a Jew to say, and it proved how true Peter was to the mind of Christ, who loved all mankind.

Then Cornelius told Peter and the whole company what had happened to him, four days ago, when he was praying, and he asked Peter to tell them what had been commanded him by God. Peter began by confessing that he had learned a new truth, and he said, " Of a truth I perceive that God is no respecter of persons : but in every nation he that feareth Him, and worketh righteousness, is accepted with Him." Then he went on to teach them that Jesus had revealed God as the Father of all men, and that He had come from God, and had gone about doing good, and healing all that were oppressed of the devil. With deeper feeling, he told them that Jesus had been crucified, but that God had raised Him from the dead, and that they, who were His disciples, had seen Jesus and spoken with Him.

Then he looked round upon them all, and said, " It is He which was ordained of God to be the Judge of quick and dead : to Him give all the prophets witness, that, through His name, whosoever believeth in Him shall receive remission of sins." While he spoke, Cornelius and his friends were moved by God's Spirit, and they believed in Jesus. The Christian men who accompanied Peter from Joppa were astonished to hear these Gentiles praising the God of Israel. Peter saw how true and sincere they were, so he baptized them in the name of Jesus. They were so eager to hear Peter speak that they begged him to stay with them for some time, to tell them more about Jesus.

It was a great day for the world, when Jews and Gentiles sat down together in a loving fellowship. It was a forecast of that time, which is coming, when every knee shall bow in the name of Jesus, and every tongue confess Him Lord.

PETER DELIVERED FROM PRISON

For some time the Christian people were allowed to live in peace. But the Jews still watched them with unrelenting hate. When the Roman Emperor appointed a new governor, named Herod Agrippa, over the whole land, a fresh persecution broke out. Herod saw that he would gain favour with the Jews if he dealt hardly with the followers of Jesus. So he slew James, the brother of John, with the sword, and he cast Peter into prison.

This happened a few days before the feast of the Passover. Jerusalem was crowded with strangers, and Herod saw that it would not be prudent to put Peter on his trial at such a time. So Peter was kept in prison, guarded by soldiers until the Passover feast had been observed.

The followers of Jesus were much distressed and saddened by this evil act. They betook themselves to unceasing prayer for Peter's deliverance. Upon the very night before Peter was to be set on his trial by Herod, he was sleeping calmly between the two soldiers to whom he was bound by chains, and other two soldiers were keeping guard at the door of the prison. Suddenly, a bright light shone in the darkness of his dungeon, and an angel aroused Peter from his sleep, and said to him, "Arise up quickly." The angel helped him to rise, and at once the chains fell off from his hands. Then the angel bade him put on his girdle, and bind his sandals on his feet, and gather his cloak about him, to follow him out of the prison.

Now Peter, awakened out of his deep slumber, and finding himself free from his chains, while the two soldiers still lay asleep, thought that this must be a dream. But as he followed the angel out of the dungeon, and passed on to the outer prison, and then to the iron gate, which was standing wide open, into the city street, he found that his deliverance was a reality and not a dream. The angel led him along one street and into another, so as to be out of sight and call by the soldiers who guarded him, if they should awake. Then the angel vanished out of his sight.

It was at a late hour of the night that Peter made his escape. The moon was shining brightly in the clear heavens over his head, and Peter stood still for a while in the shadow of the high buildings of the city, to think it all over. Then, when he had come to himself, he said, " Now I know of a surety that the Lord hath sent His angel, and hath delivered me out of the hand of Herod, and from all the expectation of the people of the Jews." He was not sure where he should go to be safe, but he remembered Mary, the mother of Mark, who wrote the Gospel of St. Mark, and he knew that she had a house where he would find a welcome. He stole through the quiet streets, and stood at the door of the porch of Mary's house.

Now the Christian people had begun to lose hope for Peter as he lay, day after day, in the prison, but they never ceased to pray for his deliverance. That same night a number of them had met in Mary's house to entreat God to restore Peter to them. As they were praying, they heard the knocking at the door of the porch. Rhoda, Mary's young maid, was sent to ask who was knocking. When she heard Peter's voice she was so excited that she ran back to the company to say that Peter was there.

They could not believe this to be true, and they said to Rhoda that she had lost her senses. But she constantly maintained that she was sure that the voice she heard was the voice of Peter. Then they said to each other, " It is his angel," for they believed at that time that every one had a guardian spirit attending him, and they thought that Peter had been put to death and his guardian angel had come to tell them. But the knocking continued and grew louder, so they opened the door, and Peter stepped in.

Peter was received with exclamations of thanksgiving and delight. But he was afraid that some of the soldiers might now be searching for him. So he lifted his hand, and hushed their voices, and told them how the Lord had brought him out of the prison. He asked them to go at once and tell the other apostles, and then he left Mary's house for another, where he would find a safe shelter.

The guard of soldiers in the prison did not discover until daylight came that Peter had escaped. They were mystified and troubled as they searched the prison and its courts. When Herod sent a messenger to tell them to bring forth Peter to his trial, they had to confess that he was gone. Herod was very angry, and called the soldiers before him to question them. He thought that either they had been careless, or had taken a bribe, and so he cruelly put them to death.

Peter knew that Herod would take every means in his power to seize him again, and that he could not stay in Jerusalem. So he left the city and went to Cæsarea where he had so many friends. While he remained in Cæsarea, teaching the believers in Jesus, an awful fate overtook Herod. He allowed the people to set him on a throne, and to make a great speech to them. They cried out, " It is the voice of a god, and not of a man ! " Then God smote him, and a foul disease fastened on his flesh, and he died.

PAUL AT PHILIPPI

After Paul had become a devoted believer in Jesus he was filled with a deep longing to tell the whole world the good news of salvation. He resolved to be a missionary, and he made journeys through many lands preaching the gospel. He began to pray that the wise and powerful nations, with their great cities across the seas, should hear of Jesus, and he asked God to show him how to go and preach to them.

In the course of one of his missionary journeys, along with two friends, Silas and Luke, he came to a little seaport town, named Troas. It looked out on the sea across to Greece and Macedonia. One night as he was praying, he saw, in a vision, a man from Macedonia standing before him. He knew him to be a man of Macedonia by the way in which he was dressed. This man begged him, "Come over into Macedonia and help us." In the morning he told his dream to his companions, and they all became sure that the Lord had called them to preach the gospel to the people of Europe.

They set sail and landed at Neapolis, which was the seaport of Philippi, the chief city of the district, where the Roman government had stationed a band of soldiers. They climbed up the high road that leads to Philippi from the coast, and passed, obscure and unknown strangers, into the city.

Now there were not many Jews in Philippi, so that they had no synagogue. But a few women used to meet for prayer in a quiet spot beside the river. Paul heard of this meeting, and he went out on the Sabbath, with his two companions, and spoke to them about Jesus. One of the women, whose name was Lydia, was not a Jewess, but she no longer worshipped the gods of the heathen, and she had come to believe in the true and living God. As Paul spoke, God opened her heart, and as she gave earnest heed to his teaching, she yielded herself to Christ, and was baptized, with all her household.

Lydia was a warm-hearted and most kindly woman. She had a good business, and she had a large house. So she begged Paul and his friends to come and be her guests. She said to them, in her gracious invitation, "If ye have judged me to be faithful to the Lord, come into my house, and abide there." They felt that she was almost too kind, but at last she constrained them to lodge with her.

Some few days afterwards, as they were going out to the place where they met for prayer, a poor, distracted slave girl began to follow them, crying out, "These men are the servants of the Most High God, which show unto us the way of salvation." This distressed girl was supposed to be able, in her excited states, to foretell fortunes, and her masters made money by allowing people to believe that she knew what was going to happen to them in the future. Paul was deeply sorry for her, and he was grieved that, day after day, she cried out as she followed them. So he turned, one day, and said to the evil spirit, "I command thee, in the name of Jesus Christ, to come out of her." At once her frenzy ceased, and she came to her right mind in quietness and gentleness.

But her masters saw that all hope of their gain was gone, and they were in a rage. They laid hold on Paul and Silas, and brought them to the market-place, and charged them before the magistrates, saying, "These men, being Jews, do exceedingly trouble our city, and teach customs which are not lawful for us to receive, neither to observe, being Romans." This roused the multitude. Then the magistrates, to please the multitude, tore off the clothes of Paul and Silas, and commanded that they should be beaten with the lash. They were then cast into prison, and the jailor of the prison was charged to keep them safely. To make sure that they would not escape, he thrust them into the dark dungeon of the inner prison, and made their feet fast in the stocks.

How well might Paul and Silas think hard thoughts even of God, and begin to wonder if God cared for them! They sat in the darkness, with backs torn and bleeding, without light or food, and the chilling damp of the dungeon made their wounds smart with a keener pain. Yet, when all in the prison were asleep, at the midnight hour, they prayed, and then they began to sing hymns of praise to God. In the silence their voices rang through the whole prison, and the other prisoners heard and wondered. But, as they were singing, there came a great earthquake. The foundations of the prison were shaken, the walls cracked, the door opened, and the rings to which the prisoners' chains were fastened were loosened.

The jailor awoke in fear. When he saw the prison doors wide open, he thought that the prisoners had escaped, and that he would be punished by death. But Paul cried with a loud voice, " Do thyself no harm ; for we are all here." The jailor was relieved, and called for a light and sprang into the prison, and fell down before Paul and Silas. He brought them out, now convinced that they were messengers of God, and he asked, " Sirs, what must I do to be saved ? "

That was the one question Paul loved to answer.

As he told him of Jesus, the jailor believed, with all his household. That same night he washed their wounds, and brought them into his own house, and set them down at his table, and gave them refreshing food.

In the morning the magistrates, who had begun to see that they had done a grievous wrong in beating men without a fair trial, sent a message to the jailor to let them go. But Paul felt that such a wrong should not be glossed over. He knew that he was a Roman citizen, and that no magistrate should use a Roman citizen in such a way. When the magistrates heard that he was a citizen of the empire, they were terrified, and they came and entreated Paul to say no more about it, and to leave the city lest the multitude should do them harm. So Paul and Silas bade Lydia and the other believers farewell, and left Philippi.

PAUL AT ROME

With the wounds of their stripes still unhealed, Paul and Silas left Philippi. Paul's sufferings had only strengthened his keen desire to preach Christ to all men. He passed on to Thessalonica, then to Athens, and then to Corinth. But Rome was the capital of the empire and the centre of the world. He longed to win Rome for Christ. So Paul said with intense feeling, " I must see Rome."

The way to Rome was opened to him after a manner

he did not expect.   He returned to Jerusalem from his journeys to find that the Jewish hatred of him had become a fury.   They charged him with stirring up the nations against them, and against their religion, and they declared that he had defiled their temple by taking Greeks into it.   These charges inflamed the minds of the people, and set Jerusalem in an uproar. Paul was seized and beaten by the mob, so the governor of the city sent a band of soldiers, who laid hold on Paul, and he was cast into prison bound by a double chain.

He was tried several times before many judges, but none of them found any fault in him.   The rulers wished to please the Jews, so he was not set free. One ruler, whose name was Felix, left him neglected for two years in prison.   The ruler who followed Felix, Festus by name, commanded Paul to be brought down to him to Cæsarea.   He listened to the charges made by the Jews, and he said that Paul ought to be tried in Jerusalem.   But Paul was not willing to be tried in Jerusalem, because of the deep hatred for him there.   He told Festus the story of his life from the days when he was a bitter young Pharisee to the present time, when he was hated because he preached that Jesus, whom the Jews crucified, was the Lord who had risen from the dead.

When Festus, along with another judge named Agrippa, was about to send him to Jerusalem, Paul resolved to declare to them that, although he was born of a Hebrew family, he was a citizen of the

Roman Empire. That meant that he had a right to be tried before a Roman judge, and to be condemned only by Roman laws. So when Festus, willing to do the Jews a pleasure, said, "Wilt thou go up to Jerusalem, and there be judged of these things before me?" Paul answered, "I stand at Cæsar's judgment seat, where I ought to be judged : to the Jews have I done no wrong, as thou very well knowest. For if I be an offender, or have committed anything worthy of death, I refuse not to die ; but if there be none of these things whereof these accuse me, no man may deliver me unto them. I appeal to the Emperor at Rome." This appeal Festus could not deny. So Paul, who had hoped to go to Rome as an apostle of Jesus Christ, went as a prisoner.

A small vessel was leaving Cæsarea to call at the seaport towns along the coast of Asia Minor. Paul and some other prisoners, who were being sent to Rome, were placed under the charge of a centurion, named Julius, with a band of soldiers, and were marched down to the harbour, and placed on board the vessel. Two of Paul's friends, Aristarchus and Luke, because of the deep affection they had for Paul, resolved to accompany him. After some days of sailing they were transferred to a larger ship which was going to Rome. It was greatly overcrowded, for it was packed with two hundred and seventy-six passengers.

The captain of this vessel set out on his voyage with some misgiving. The winter was coming on, and the time for safe and pleasant sailing was past. He made up his mind not to go far on his way, but to pass the winter in some safe harbour in the Island of Crete. But the weather continued to be fair and beautiful, and he sailed farther on. Then a sudden and terrific storm burst upon them. The vessel was

A sudden and terrific storm burst upon them.

driven helplessly before the howling blasts, and the waves broke over her, until the captain and the sailors began to fear that she would sink. To lighten the ship they threw the cargo overboard, and then they cast out the furniture. But the storm continued in its fury, and all hope of being saved was taken away.

Then Paul, who had kept silent, stood forth and spoke to the dejected captain and sailors, and to the despairing passengers. " I exhort you," he said, " to be of good cheer : for there shall be no loss of any man's life among you, only of the ship. For there stood by me this night the angel of God, whose I am, and whom I serve, saying, Fear not, Paul ; thou must be brought before Cæsar : and, lo, God hath given thee all them that sail with thee."

As they listened to Paul's cheering message they were encouraged and comforted. But the furious winds still smote on the vessel, and she was driven, now this way and now that way, no one knew where. On the fourteenth night of the storm, about midnight, the sailors heard the surf beating on some shore. They took soundings to find the depth of the water, and they learned that it was shallowing. They were afraid they might be dashed on some rocky coast, so that not one of them would escape. They cast four anchors out of the stern, which held the vessel, and began to wish eagerly for the coming of the morning light.

As these anchors steadied the ship, Paul spoke to the passengers, when he saw how weary and how faint with hunger they were. They had eaten nothing for many days, so he besought them to take some food. He did not forget to witness to his faith in God. He himself took some bread, but, before he began to eat, he gave God thanks. When the captain and the centurion and the other passengers saw how brave and calm Paul was, they were strengthened and cheered.

When the day dawned, they made out the land; but they did not know where they were. But they saw, with thankfulness, that it was not a rocky shore. So they took up the anchors and allowed the ship to be driven in on the beach. When she grounded, the onrush of the waves beat upon the stern of the vessel and began to break her up. But as they were not far from the shore, some cast themselves into the sea and swam to the beach. Others were carried on planks and broken pieces of the ship, and so they all escaped safe to land.

These shipwrecked men learned that they had landed on the island of Malta. The islanders were not Greeks, but they showed them great kindness, and Paul was soon recognised as a man who could be respected. He earned their gratitude by healing Publius, the chief man of the island, who lay sick of a fever. The whole company remained in Malta for the remaining three months of the winter. Then they found a ship which was sailing to Italy, and they took passage in it to go to Rome.

They sailed through the Straits of Messina, touched at Syracuse, and landed at Puteoli, a seaport which is one hundred and forty miles from Rome. Here they found, to Paul's great joy, a little gathering of believers in Christ. They received Paul and his companions with a cordial welcome. He was well known, as he had written a letter to the Christians in Rome. They entreated him to stay seven days with them. But Paul was a prisoner, and although Julius, the centurion, had a deep respect and affection for Paul, it was not in his power to allow a prisoner to wait so long a time.

So Julius and his band of soldiers marched Paul and the other prisoners, accompanied by Aristarchus and Luke, along the famous Appian Road that leads to Rome. The news that Paul was coming had already reached the believers in the city. Some of them came out to meet him at the Appian Market, which is about forty miles from the city. A second company met him at the Three Taverns, ten miles farther on. Paul was gladdened and comforted by their welcome. He had been thinking sad thoughts, as he drew near this heathen city, with its godless rulers. But when he saw these fellow-believers, and heard their words of welcome, he thanked God and took courage.

Then Paul entered Rome. The centurion, Julius, showed him great kindness, for he was not cast into a prison among a crowd of criminals. He was allowed for some time to live in his own hired house, with only one soldier on guard at the door. Some of the Roman Christians came to him, and even Jews to whom he spoke of Jesus were admitted to see him. After some delay he was taken before the Emperor Nero—one of the most wicked and most cruel men the world has known. But he was never set free, and, at last, he was slain by the sword and died as a martyr to Christ. Yet in his prison he wrote many wonderful letters, and as we read them we can hear his voice sounding forth the old, old story of love and the power of Jesus Christ his Lord.

To the Uttermost Part of the Earth

When we tell this old, old story of Jesus and His love, we are led back to the places whose names are so dear that they will never be forgotten. We go to Bethlehem and its manger-cradle ; to Nazareth and its carpenter's shop ; to Jerusalem and its green hill far away, where the dear Lord was crucified ; to the garden and its grave out of which Jesus came forth in His glory ; and to Bethany where He spoke His last words of farewell. Then we travel along the great roads, and across the wide seas, until we come to Rome, where Paul laid down his life for His Lord.

But no disciple, not even Peter or John, Paul or Luke, foresaw how far abroad this old, old story would be told. There are lands, where to-day the name of Jesus is above every name, that were quite unknown to them. There are peoples who rejoice in God and His Son, Jesus Christ, whom they never heard of. No one of these disciples even dreamed of the languages in which the story would be repeated, or of the new songs in which His praise would be sung. But Jesus knew. He said to the little company, as He bade them farewell, " Ye shall be witnesses unto me both in Jerusalem, and in all

Judea, and in Samaria, and to the uttermost part of the earth."

Now let us take a map of the whole world, and spread it out until all its countries lie open before our eyes. Let us trace the footprints of the missionaries who went out to be witnesses to Jesus. It will be a lesson, not only in geography and in history, but, if we care to go on, in a wonderful arithmetic. We shall not only learn the names of the people, and read the story of their doings, often so sad, and of their decline and fall, but we shall see that only where these witnesses to Jesus have gone, is there peace on earth and goodwill to men. We shall become sure that wherever there is war, and hatred, and cruelty, and greed, or wherever there are wrongs that are full of shame, it is because the witnesses have not yet reached these heathen lands, or because they have not believed the old, old story they have been told.

Now, as we look at this map of the world, what do we see ? We see the continuation of the story which was begun in the book of the Acts of the Apostles. We see men and women passing out among all nations, because Jesus has sent them. Here is a small company going up to Antioch, and then making their way into the wilds of Russia. Here is another turning their faces to the south, and going down to Egypt, and passing along the coasts of Africa. Here is another setting out from Constantinople, to speak to the wild tribes in the heart of Europe. Here is another leaving Rome, going up through Italy into the Swiss valleys, and then travelling to the south along the river Rhone, and making their way to the north by the banks of the Rhine.   Of this company one little band finds the sunny plains of France, and another the great forests of Germany, to tell the same story to the rude and pitiless people that dwelt in them. Then we see a very few of these witnesses looking across at the white cliffs at Dover, making their passage in little ships, and travelling through England across to Ireland, and then to Scotland, with the same message of the love of God in Christ Jesus.

But there is a sad line in this record.   For long years these words of Jesus were forgotten.   Perhaps it was because the people had no Bibles in their hands. But at least they were remembered.   Then again men and women went forth making long journeys by land and by sea, and in weariness and painfulness, facing hardship and loneliness, and death, to tell the story of the cross.   To India, to China, to Africa, to the islands of the sea, they carried the good news of the gospel of Christ.

What do we learn as we follow the trail of these witnesses ?   We are taught that theirs is the pathway of the conquerors over sin and shame, misery and fear.   They found men brutal and cruel.   They saw women as mere beasts of burden.   They heard the pitiful weeping of little children in their pain. They brought light to those who walked in darkness, and peace to men who were at strife.   New joys, new purities, new hopes, filled men's hearts and lives. The day will come when the great multitude of all nations, and kindreds, and people, and tongues shall stand before the throne. But, even then, they will not cease to tell this old, old story of Jesus and His love.